DATE DUE			

Roman London

This book gives a clear and condensed account of the tremendous activity that has been conducted for more than a century in the City of London and in the surrounding areas to re-create the Roman town of Londinium. This town, which grew far larger than the Roman Emperor Claudius ever imagined in A.D. 43, became the most important port and town of the province of Britain.

The author describes the techniques used by archaeologists to obtain information and explains the significance of the closely packed layers of soil which today lie under modern pavements and buildings. The combination of geographical factors, the demands for imports, and the flow of exports from the province caused people from many parts of the Roman Empire to converge on Londinium. Exotic sculpture and varied pottery which are not often found in other British sites are found in the levels of this area. The peculiar difficulties which have to be faced in excavation there are much more complicated than those faced in other sites in the open countryside. The human activity which has been concentrated in the small area of the City of London makes the task of the archaeologist a very rewarding but a very difficult operation.

This book will be of interest to the historian, the archaeologist, and the would-be archaeologist alike.

Also in this series

EGYPT Anne Millard
THE ROMANS Mark Hassall
THE GREEKS John Ellis Jones

THE YOUNG ARCHAEOLOGIST BOOKS
Edited by Robin Place, MA, FSA

Roman London

ILID E. ANTHONY

Drawings by Isabella Whitworth

WITH A FOREWORD BY
NORMAN COOK, BA, FSA, FMA

G. P. Putnam's Sons   New York

ISBN 0 298 79122 6
Set in 12 pt. Lumitype Times
and printed in Great Britain

Published simultaneously by
Rupert Hart-Davis Educational Publications and
G. P. Putnam's Sons, 200 Madison Avenue, New York
Library of Congress Catalog Card Number: 70-146107

Contents

List of Illustrations

Foreword

The opportunities for excavation in the City of London which were made possible by the vast areas of devastation due to the bombing during the Second World War have led to a number of discoveries which have added greatly to our knowledge of Londinium, the Roman City. The attendant publicity has raised such questions as "How do you know where to dig?" and "How do archaeologists excavate?" It is most important that these questions should be answered properly and that the difference between treasure hunting (looking for objects) and archaeological excavation (looking for information) should be made clear. For this reason I welcome this book and hope that it will lead many to a proper understanding of our work in London and perhaps, one day, provide recruits to the growing number of amateurs who find great pleasure and interest in the pursuit of archaeology.

NORMAN COOK, BA, FSA, FMA
Director, Museum of London

CHAPTER ONE

Exploring London's Past

Few people hurrying along the streets and alleyways of modern London think of the centuries of activity on the same spot on the banks of the Thames river. Yet the Romans, almost 2,000 years ago, saw the advantages of this wide impressive waterway, for trade as well as for military purposes, and built a town there, which they called Londinium. This town, which grew far larger than the Roman Emperor Claudius ever imagined in A.D. 43, became the most important port and town of the province of Britain and its unchallenged capital.

Five and a half metres of closely packed layers of soil lie under the modern pavements. These layers vary in colour and in material. When buildings have been used for a long time they need repair. They may be pulled down and larger buildings set up in their place. Each time a building is demolished and the site is levelled so that a new house can be built on top of the ruins of the old one, the ground level rises a little. So, when several centuries have passed and several buildings have been built, used, and then pulled down, a considerable depth of debris will be formed. In this way, the thick layers between the Roman Londinium and modern London have gradually accumulated through the centuries.

Some levels contain ash and charred timbers. These were formed when buildings were burned down long ago. Light brown soils with lumps of mortar and rubble are the remains of house walls. A mass of broken red tile and iron nails is the collapsed roof of such buildings. A pinkish mortar is often the indication of a former floor. This is what such deposits mean to archaeologists.

How levels are formed

It is not always as easy as this to "read" the meaning of deposits. Layers do not always lie flat, one above another. They may be cut into by pits, well shafts, natural stream beds, and so on. Pits are the most common interruption of a layer. Think of

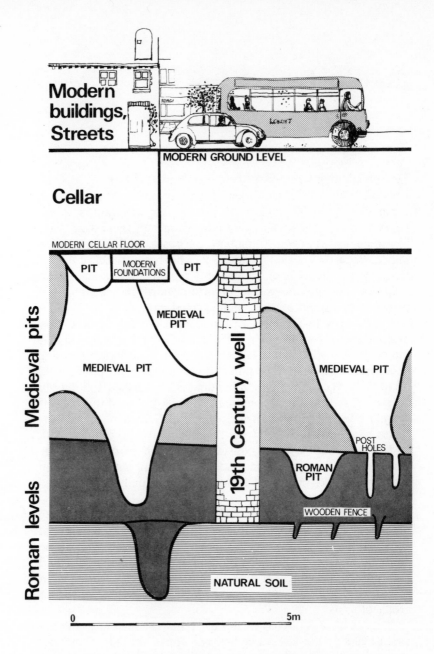

A section to show how levels have been accumulated above each other both in the Roman period and afterwards up into modern times.

many people living in a settlement, all eating joints of meat, breaking pottery, and generally accumulating rubbish. Then there was no garbage collection every week. So people dug pits and gradually filled them up with their rubbish.

Although the Romans usually planned drainage channels for most of their larger buildings and houses, some of the smaller buildings had cesspits near them. These pits with their characteristic dark, slimy filling offer further complications in such a densely populated town as London. Wells might run dry or become polluted, and the shaft would then be filled with rubbish.

This activity of digging pits continued to be a feature of the medieval town which followed the Roman period. The houses were concentrated within the city wall. Large numbers of people lived in tightly packed houses. From the sixteenth century on buildings were constructed outside the town walls, but this did not stop the custom of disposing of rubbish in pits. All archaeological excavators in London have to be ready to note these pits and to detect the level in which the "lip," or top, of a

Roman timber-lined well with orange earthenware jug emerging in the filling. Queen Street.

pit occurs so that it can be put into its correct century or period.

Each layer or pit filling contains such objects as coins, iron nails, bronze brooches or other jewelry, and all sorts of things made by man for his use. (This applies to all levels, not only to the Roman.) These items are the clues to and evidence of the date when that layer began to form and the area was occupied. The items are sometimes associated with foundations of buildings. These foundation walls are exposed to provide a plan of houses, temples, shops, and other structures.

To the careful excavator all these things provide information about what London looked like in Roman and later times. The objects are the clues that indicate the date of each building layer. The archaeologist can talk about the first Roman London, a town of warehouses and dwellings, which were erected in the first century soon after A.D. 43, when the Romans began to occupy Britain. The timber buildings can be dated to this time because near them were found coins of the Emperors Claudius (A.D. 42–54) and Nero (A.D. 54–68).

Stratification of evidence   A red layer approximately 30 centimeters thick was caused by the attack of the natives led by Boudicca (or Boadicea) in A.D. 61, when Roman London was burned to the ground. The date of this burned level would have been evident, even if the account of a Roman author describing the destruction had not survived. Foundations of new buildings above this black level had been built in the second century A.D. because coins and pottery of that time were found with them.

In many ways these different levels are like the layers of a cake. The objects dropped in them are like the chopped nuts or chocolate in the cake layers. The trouble is that the levels in a site like London are not as distinct and level as those in a cake. Also, even the whole "cake" sank below the water level. It is a fact explained by geologists that in the second century A.D. the southeast of Britain was slowly sinking. The Roman citizens of London felt the effects of this when wharves and nearby buildings and streets were frequently flooded by the Thames river. They had to bring soil, rubble, and gravel in to lay down over the flooded area and then start to build all over again. Imagine the problems posed to the archaeologists as a result of these activities.

Bronze toilet set from the site of the Walbrook stream.

12   After Roman London was founded, it expanded with unexpected success until it extended over 44 hectares. It was

occupied until well into the fifth century A.D. by citizens who understood the Roman way of organizing a town, although that methodical system became less efficient as time went on. A change of people brought new ideas and new methods of administration. Many of the early buildings were in ruins, and Norman and other builders erected their structures directly on top of the ruined walls of Roman buildings. Very often they destroyed many rooms, monuments, and streets in the course of their work. Because many more people came to live in London, wells had to be sunk to get water for them. Sewers were dug to carry waste waters away to London's rivers. These wells and sewers and many rubbish pits were often dug through the neat floors of the Roman buildings. Norman and medieval defenders of the city restored the Roman town wall but put a number of new stones and tiles into the holes and ruined sections.

In 1666 the Fire of London destroyed a very large area of the city. This caused another thick black level to form much higher than the black level caused by the fire of Boudicca in A.D. 61. As we shall see, this gave the inhabitants of the seventeenth century an opportunity to build a better and larger city. It was also a time when many discoveries of the Roman period could have been made, if anyone had been interested.

Then for the first time buildings were put up beyond the *Roads from* Roman and medieval city wall. This growth still continues *London* today, so that London extends into Middlesex on the north and into Surrey on the south. Today London has spread far along all the Roman roads that were laid out from Londinium, so that traffic from the town could travel to other centers. Later scholars have given names to some of these roads.

Watling Street was built from Londinium along the north coast of Kent to Rutupiae (Richborough). From the center of the town to the north through modern Stanmore the road continued to Sulloniacae (Brockley Hill) and Verulamium (St. Albans).

One of the earliest roads to be laid was the one to Camulodonum (Colchester) since that was the most important town in the southeast before the Romans came.

Stane Street ran south across the Weald of Sussex to Noviomagus (Chichester). This allowed the iron of that area and other products of the countryside to be brought to Londinium.

Ermine Street was a very important road that ran north to 13

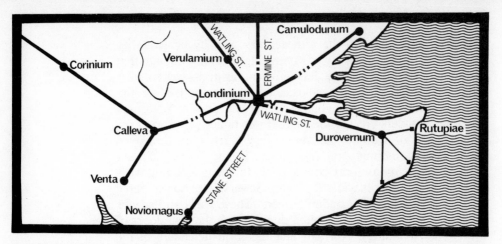

Durovigutum (Godmanchester) and eventually to Lindum (Lincoln).

The main road to the west ran from Londinium to Calleva (Silchester), a Roman town near modern Reading, and from there to Aquae Sulis (Bath).

Some of these roads are still the busiest routes out of London. We shall see that the gates through which they left the walled town continued to be well-known places throughout the medieval period.

It was this combination of good roads with a good port that made Roman London a successful town. Invaders had penetrated up the Thames Valley long before Julius Caesar in 54 B.C., but they were bands of settlers looking for land to cultivate for their small farms.

As a military commander pursuing the native leader Cassivellaunus, Caesar was primarily concerned with taking his troops across the Thames. Did he notice the stretch of hard-packed sand that extends out from the area of modern Southwark toward another mass of gravel on the opposite bank—the area of the modern City of London? This area is defined on the map on page 15 and is the original commercial center still active today and under the authority of the Lord Mayor.

We have no proof of the spot where Caesar crossed the river or even of the position of the tremendous battle which took place in A.D. 43 between the legions of Claudius and the native tribes. But because of the choice of site for the town that came later, it is probable that Claudius and his army crossed the river somewhere near the site of the Old London Bridge (this was 28.5

14

meters east of the present bridge). The exact position has not yet been found because of changes in the course of the river. But one of the first things the new settlers would have erected would have been a bridge and storehouses near the spot where the successful crossing had been made. It would be very interesting if the remains of such wooden structures could be found with coins of Claudius (A.D. 42–54) or Nero (A.D. 54–68) to date them.

WHAT DID THE SITE OF LONDON LOOK LIKE WHEN THE FIRST ROMANS CAME?

Two small rivers flowed into the Thames from the bank on the north opposite Southwark. One was the Fleet, which flowed from the high ground at Hampstead, through the course of Farringdon Street, to enter the Thames at Blackfriars.

The second, called Walbrook, flowed down from Hoxton, west of the modern street called Walbrook, and Cannon Street to enter the Thames near Cannon Street Station.

There were two hills, very low ones only approximately 15

Plan of Londinium showing the river Thames, the streams and the fort as well as the course of the city wall.

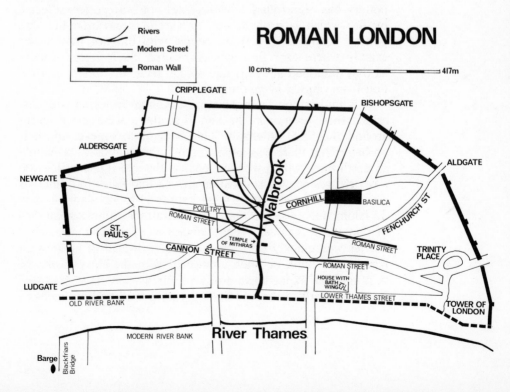

meters high, which stood on either side of the Walbrook stream. The one on the east is called Cornhill today, and the one on the west is Ludgate; the Roman town extended approximately 3 kilometers along the bank of the Thames—it became an almost rectangular shape with the river passing along the long southern side.

Another settlement appears to have grown upon the natural gravel where Westminster stands today. A third area where Roman finds have been discovered is between Southwark and Camberwell. A very large number of Roman objects have been dredged up from the riverbed in the neighborhood of London Bridge. This is why it is thought that the Roman bridge was erected there. Probably during the course of 400 years there was more than one bridge—each on a different site. Plenty of finds—brooches, coins, sandals, and other objects—in the riverbeds during random excavations prove that many people lived by the rivers Fleet and Walbrook.

Area of first settlement of London
The exact boundary of the first settlement is not precisely known. More work in the central area will show the limit of that heavily burned level caused by the destruction of A.D. 61. A very clever piece of detective work has already been done by putting marks on a map of London to show where burned pottery has been found. This includes not only pottery affected by fire which is brought out by careful excavation but also pottery found long ago by people who did not write down exactly where each find was discovered. Such detective work as that described above is one way of trying to obtain information from objects in museums.

It is understood from Tacitus, a Roman historian who described these events in Britain, that there were no defenses around the first settlement. This is hard to believe, and it is probable that there was a barrier, though it may have been only an earth bank with a wooden fence at the top. It is possible that any defenses erected soon after A.D. 43 had fallen into ruins by A.D. 61. This seems to be what happened to Verulamium only 32 kilometres away, so that when the attack came, a great deal of damage was done. When London was attacked, any flimsy barrier was quickly overcome. So now, instead of looking for traces of a bank or ditch connected with the early town, the best method might be to study the areas that have produced burned pottery of the mid-first-century period and put a dotted

16

line around it to indicate the size and possible area of the first Roman London and its defenses.

A small fort was erected in the early century to the northwest of the settlement. At the end of the second century this was enclosed within the line of the town wall and main defense system. This was a stone wall that made a definite change of direction to incorporate the north and west walls of the fort. Sections dug across the defenses showed two foundations side by side. The fort wall was only 120.4 centimeters wide, and when the town wall touched its northeastern corner, another foundation was added to the inner side to make the whole up to $2\frac{1}{2}$ or 3 meters wide to be in keeping with the rest.

The levels of the fourth century A.D. in London have been greatly damaged by the activity of later builders digging deeply into them. Archaeologists are always on the lookout for small pits or some surviving inscription, perhaps on a milestone or altar, that may fill the gaps in the story of Londinium. Coins fortunately are hard and do not break. We have evidence that there was a mint in London toward the end of the third century. We also have some information from written history which refers to the restoration of London by Constantius Chlorus and later by another general, Theodosius, in the middle of the fourth century. It is possible that the site of Londinium was never deserted and that immediate rebuilding was partly responsible for the small number of late buildings found up to the present time.

HOW DO ARCHAEOLOGISTS FIND OUT ABOUT ROMAN LONDON?

The main source of information is the observation of innumerable trenches dug for the foundations of new buildings or when sewers, electricity cables, or gas pipes are being laid. The field officers from the London and Guildhall museums are continually being called out to watch such undertakings in case some new piece of evidence is revealed in the trenches, even if no further exploration is possible.

Archaeologists are often compared to detectives who are called to solve a case after a crime has been committed. Most people know that no one must touch anything at all anywhere near the scene of the crime. Unfortunately because of natural causes, such as floods, weathering—that is, the action of wind, 17

(*Opposite*) Mr. Peter Marsden, of the Guildhall Museum, excavating the Roman barge at Blackfriars in 1963. The large timbers fastened by large iron nails are shown. The square mast-step is seen at the center beneath the modern girder, an unfinished millstone is seen to the right of the same girder at the top.

Mast-step of the Roman barge at the Blackfriars Bridge excavation with coin in position before the mast itself was inserted.

rain, and frost on buildings—and, above all, man's activity over the centuries the clues here often become confused.

Yet much can be deduced by very careful observation of the exact position of each item that comes to light and its exact relation to the Roman floors above or below it or to pits and pillars nearby. When the field officers and their helpers are called out, they have to work quickly to make section drawings that is, accurate plans of the levels as they lie one above the other. They must draw plans of the layout of buildings if they are fortunate enough to have a large section to examine. More often the trenches are small and only fragments of the buildings are seen. This is why the plan of Londinium still looks incomplete. In 1888 Henry Hodge, an observer, described foundations and impressive tiled vaulting near Leadenhall market. This was part of the Roman basilica or town hall, and several other observers have since added to our knowledge of this important building.

Observing levels

Foundations for a gantry at Blackfriars were constructed in 1962, and, when piers were being driven down into the deep mud of the riverbanks, part of a Roman barge was found. It was carefully excavated by Peter Marsden of the Guildhall Museum. A year later, when a cofferdam was built for the construction of a new embankment wall, it was possible to excavate more of the barge. A coin of the Emperor Domitian

Discovery of timber barge

19

was then found under the mast lying on the mast step. Inside the hold of the barge was found some Kentish rag, a type of stone quarried near Maidstone. From this find we know where the builders of the town wall and other structures obtained their materials and how they were transported to London. A very full investigation of the barge was carried out by Marsden and others, and the information was incorporated in the report written afterward.

FORMER EXPLORERS INTO THE ANTIQUITIES OF LONDON

Before the twentieth century there were many difficulties in unraveling the history and layout of Roman London. Those interested in its past had to learn how to observe the evidence which appeared in pits and trenches in the ground. There were no professional archaeologists or textbooks to tell them what to do. At first these observers did not describe the color of the soil in which the objects lay. They did not look to see if there was a wall or pavement near the find. As time passed and the opportunity for looking under the pavements of London became more frequent, the record became better and fuller, until today all interested in this subject learn the rules and the methods before they dig. They also sometimes find that they have the opportunity to dig deliberately to answer certain specific questions about a site.

Early discoveries In 1595 a gentleman called Stowe wrote of a pavement which he discovered 4.5 meters below the ground level of his time. It was one of the earliest records of this important fact—namely, that the rubbish and foundations of former generations lie under later ones that were piled above them.

During the seventeenth century scholars became aware of the antiquities to be found in the ground in their own countries. This was the result of the New Learning, the Renaissance, which made many people curious about the past as well as about other aspects of learning.

Since they were very anxious to acquire objects, they were mainly interested in burials. The "grave goods," or objects placed in the graves with the dead, were much more likely to be undamaged than objects from pits containing rubbish. It was also easier to excavate and understand simple burials than the complicated relationship of floors and walls.

20

Jugs and a glass vessel from a fourth-century grave in the Minories.

In the seventeenth century burials were found in Bishopsgate; others were found near the Old Bailey and St. Martin-le-Grand. Today we realize that the burials in the Roman period were always placed outside the walls of the settlements. When they are found within the walls of a fully developed Roman town, we know that they belonged to an early phase in the history of that place. These burials must therefore belong to the first-century town, outside an early boundary system which may one day be found, for Roman cemeteries which were used in the third century after the stone wall was built were in three main areas. In the east there was one at Aldgate High Street. Near Bishopsgate, in the north, was found a cemetery which extended to Moorgate. In the west burials were found between St. Martin-le-Grand and the Fleet stream. These cemeteries were beyond the wall of the later Roman town; this was only found to be so after much more exploration.

Cemeteries outside the walls

THE GREAT FIRE AND THE OPPORTUNITY TO EXCAVATE

A wonderful opportunity to dig beneath the crowded buildings which had been swept away occurred after the Great Fire of 21

London in 1666. Unfortunately, the new spirit of inquiry was not sufficiently widespread to encourage people to make full use of this opportunity. It was three centuries later before a similar chance occurred to explore the history of London. This came in World War II, when the bombs of 1940 devastated so much of the center of modern London.

After the fire of 1666 Sir Christopher Wren was appointed "Surveyor General and Principal Architect" with the tremendous task of rebuilding St. Paul's Cathedral and the area around it. He was far too preoccupied with his many duties and the difficulties to give much attention to historical research. However, in spite of many obstacles, he found time to write about pottery kilns found under the site of St. Paul's and also of Roman burials which were discovered during the reconstruction. Of the foundations and the road surfaces which must have appeared, there is little information.

In a complicated town such as London it is most important to determine where the natural surface was before the Romans came. From this knowledge the levels accumulated above are understood more quickly. For instance, many more levels and buildings can be found nearer the river than up on the higher ground where the modern buildings have caused more damage by digging more drastically into the Roman levels. Imagine a period when no one had thought out this logical problem of where the natural surface of the ground, the starting point of the story, was.

One of the most important questions for any archaeologist— and one, therefore, which he must always be able to answer—is: Where is the natural soil? When a digger works in a level that does not produce objects or foundations, it is possible that he has reached the natural or undisturbed soil. This is not always so simple. An archaeologist has to know a little about geological formations in order to recognize when to stop. He must learn especially what deposits to look for in river valleys and to recognize small side streams, such as the Fleet and the Walbrook.

Archaeologists are grateful to the notes made about a stream bed near St. Lawrence Jewry by Sir Christopher Wren and others who rebuilt churches after the Great Fire of 1666. Following this deduction the position of other stream beds, subsequently filled in, have been noted. The natural color of the soil was described in many places. Under the tower of St. Mary-le-

Bow the gravel surface of a Roman street was observed. This was the first of many such references which have helped build up the map of the street system of Londinium.

After Wren's rebuilding, the next burst of activity below the streets of London came when improved drainage was planned for the expanding city in the late eighteenth and early nineteenth centuries. Sewers were dug under the modern streets. Again, no one in authority was sufficiently interested to plot any of the discoveries that were made when channels were being dug.

Several individuals, however, made reports on what they saw. Two such people were A. J. Kemp and W. Herbert, who published their reports in *Archaeologia* and *The Gentleman's Magazine*. Specialized journals of this kind had been concerned with the study of antiquities since the eighteenth century, and scholars today often consult these early observations. *Discoveries made during the laying of modern sewers*

The channels for the newly constructed sewers were often laid under the modern streets. In old streets iron manholes indicate that a sewer runs below the carriageway. Therefore, finds were made under the nineteenth-century road surfaces, and often Roman masonry walls and floors could be seen to cross the line of the modern street. This showed that the Roman streets did not exactly underlie the modern ones. One exception to this was the discovery, at the eastern end of Lombard Street, of the gravel surface of a Roman road. This street ran in the same east–west direction as the modern road. It was so deep down and had been resurfaced so many times that it seems to have been a road since the earliest settlement in London. This would make it one of the earliest streets in Britain.

Many people think of archaeological digging as a treasure hunt. This view of the work was much more general during the past two centuries than it is today. Today we do not think of digging simply as a way to obtain Roman pottery, glass, and coins. When we find them, we think more of where we found them and what they can tell us about the building or the street or ditch. Although we are sad that the interested men who reported on finds during the work of laying sewer channels did not always see enough and write enough about what they saw, we must be grateful that they made as many notes as they did. Their aim was largely to collect objects to put into drawers and into glass cases.

Five major collections of Roman objects were formed during 23

Marble statue of the river god found in the Walbrook area
in 1889.

the operation when laborers dug channels in every street for the
sewers. Unscrupulous dealers would buy anything that these
laborers found. They were not interested in the exact findspot of
each object. "Findspot" is the term used to describe exactly
where an object has been found. Its depth from the modern surface, its relationship to a pavement or a road or the pillar of a
building are always important. Although the more scholarly
observers often listed and named the places where objects were
found, even they were not quite as thorough as the modern
archaeologists. So the story is vague when we work on the items
found during this period of the exploration of London.

One very important collector was a man called Charles
Roach Smith, an early-nineteenth-century pharmacist who,
during the days of his apprenticeship at Chichester, had become
interested in Roman objects. He realized that Roman finds
should be marked on a map, that their findspots should be plotted so there would be a permanent record. In 1834, to give himself freedom for this work, he left his business in the hands of
staff whom he could trust, so that he himself was able to spend a
great deal of time watching the sewer-laying operations. Although energetic and anxious about the lack of proper surveys
being carried out, he was not tactful in his discussions with local
authorities who ought to have helped. They were indifferent to
the destruction of ancient remains and did nothing about the
problem. Roach Smith quarreled several times with the Common Council of the City of London. Modern archaeologists
have learned that it is important to be very tactful with the
owners of sites, or they will not be given an opportunity to carry
out a proper excavation on a site.

Not only did the city authorities refuse to allow time for
proper records during the digging operations, but they were un-
gracious enough to refuse two of the large collections of the
finds from Roman levels when these were offered to them in
1824. It was only after 1841 that they eventually gave a build-
in which to house the objects found on the site of the General
Post Office when excavations were carried out there.

Meanwhile, the Roach Smith Collection continued to grow
and was shown to the public by the owner. In 1854 he published
a catalog containing a description of the antiquities. Later he
sold the collection to the British Museum, where it is today.

Another important collector was W. Ransome of Hitchin.

Among the sculptured stones which he acquired was an important relief of the god Mithras killing a bull. This was said to have come from a depth of $\frac{1}{2}$ to 6 meters, in the soil filling the valley of the Walbrook near Bond Court. Found in 1889, this relief and that of the figure of a river god, both of marble, came out of the ground while sewage works were constructed in the area. At that time a block of offices was built on the site which stood there until it was destroyed in World War II. Then, in 1952, the foundations of this bombed office block were removed, and Professor W. F. Grimes undertook an excavation of the site. This is where he found a mithraeum (a temple dedicated to the god Mithras); it must have been the building into which the relief of the god killing the bull was set.

This shows how important it is to keep a record, however brief, with a description of the surroundings in which an object is found. Many years later the fuller explanation may be forthcoming. Problems still unsolved in the story of London will perhaps be answered by the finds of the next hundred years. We shall be discussing some of these unsolved problems in Chapter Two.

The sculptured figures and reliefs collected by Ransome are in the London Museum, which is in part of Kensington Palace.

Between 1834 and 1871 the commercial activity and the bigger ships that needed to come to the port of London caused the authorities to deepen the navigation channels by dredging the mud from the bottom of the Thames. Ships with special dredgers on board carried the mud from the port area and deposited it along the banks from Barnes to Hammersmith. When this mud dried out, pottery, bronze objects, lead and iron tools, and weapons were found. This material had been dropped and lost in the streets and wooden huts along the Roman riverbank. The waters of the river had covered the area with the increased flooding mentioned above. Today groups of amateur archaeological societies (successors to the Thames Basin Observers Group) carry on a very careful watch on every bank along the river in order to find out as much as possible. They study the alluvial mud whenever they can. Their work is much better planned than that of the people 100 years ago.

THE DISCOVERY OF TIMBER BUILDINGS
IN LONDON

In the latter part of the nineteenth century more people joined in the work of watching workmen digging down into the buried

Excavation of the outside of a timber structure on the site of the
Bank of England and South America, Queen Street/Queen Victoria Street.

levels of Roman London. In 1866 a Colonel Lane-Fox helped in
the observations. Lane-Fox later had to change his name to
inherit large estates in Dorset. As General Pitt-Rivers, he
became famous for his meticulous large-scale excavations there.
In London, Lane-Fox showed his archaeological ability in his
interpretation of timber posts that were found in the old riverbed
of the Walbrook, where the ground was damp enough to have
preserved the wood. The timber, though soft, still had its shape
and form. In ordinary dry soil, wood becomes first a fiber and
then a brownish powdery substance.

People of the time were reading about the wooden piles being
found in the Swiss lake dwellings. These were about 3,000 years
older than the Roman remains. The Swiss sites seized the public
imagination, and people were ready to find traces of such
ancient dwellings beside the Thames. Fortunately Colonel Lane-
Fox believed only what he saw with his own eyes. Ignoring the
Swiss lake dwellings, he declared that the Walbrook timbers
were of the Roman period because he saw that there was
Roman pottery with them. This shows how independent and
scientific an archaeological observer must be. He must not jump 27

to a conclusion just because superficial appearances might suggest things of the wrong period and place.

THE LONDON AND MIDDLESEX ARCHAEOLOGICAL SOCIETY

The commercial activity which had caused the river to be made deeper and the sewers to be laid also caused a tremendous amount of rebuilding between 1860 and 1890. Individuals had in the main acted separately, but the interest in what had been going on in London in the past caused the London and Middlesex Society to be extremely active. One of the most industrious members was J. E. Price, who was present whenever large-scale operations were being undertaken. Price was tactful in his relations with the authorities, the builders, and the workmen; this made it easier for him to be allowed to make drawings of what he saw and to visit the building sites as often as he wanted to.

Mosaic pavement   One important discovery made about this time was a large mosaic pavement lying between Bucklersbury and Lothbury in the City. Price drew accurate plans of it and reported fully on its discovery. The general public was allowed to visit the site. This was a new event, and it is interesting to learn that people came in large numbers, showing that interest in the past was becoming more general.

THE FIRST PLANNED EXCAVATION IN THE CITY OF LONDON

The next step in progress toward understanding the layout of Roman London was to plan to dig in a certain place in order to

Drawing of the mosaic pavement found at Bucklersbury in 1869.

answer a specific question. This kind of digging did not actually happen until 1876. In that year the London and Middlesex Society paid for the hire of three workmen to clear and measure a bastion, a semicircular solid tower, which had been found in Camomile Street. The builders themselves were not going to expose it fully before covering it up again. It was obviously good that someone was going to excavate the bastion properly before it was lost again beneath the foundations of the new building.

Bastions were added by the Romans to town walls so that heavy ballistae (a ballista was a war machine) could be pushed out to hurl heavy stones at attackers. Many of the bastions have since been discovered. Some of them are medieval, but there were certainly some which were constructed by the original Roman builders. Sculptured stones were found built into the bastion; this was a frequent practice of Roman builders, who used carved or shaped stones whenever they needed a great deal of building material. One carved stone showed a Roman soldier in relief. Another was a carved head, possibly of the Roman Emperor Philip I. Both these stones were handed to the Guildhall Museum. A plan of the bastion and its exact position was recorded.

Bastions added to town walls

The largest building found in 1880 was one that lay under Leadenhall Market. The same large medieval building had stood on this spot for centuries. The floor of the market had been built on masonry arches, the pillars of which had been built deep into the soil, as concrete piles are driven down today. When these arches were removed, massive Roman foundations were found below. These wide masonry foundations formed two parallel lines that marked the site of an extensive aisled hall. This has been identified as the Roman town hall or basilica. The identification has been made more certain by discoveries which have been made since. The records of 1880 consist of plans and watercolor drawings. It was not possible then to make photographic records easily as we do today.

Basilica under Leadenhall Market

Two more patient workers, a Dr. Norman and a Mr. Reader, gave a great deal of their valuable time to the problem of the Roman town wall. Measured drawings across the wall—that is, as if a large knife had cut a slice through it as if it were a cake—are called sections. Norman and Reader's work consisted of making several section drawings of the wall. In many

29

instances only the lowest rough stones of the foundation survived. In others one or two lines of the trimmed, or dressed, stones of the wall itself appeared. When a fairly high section survived, the stones were interrupted by lines of red tile at 1- to 1.5-meter intervals as the masonry was built up.

Behind most town walls earth was piled up and sloped down from the parapet walk at the top to the street level within the town. Flights of steps were built at intervals along the bank. These allowed the defenders to come down to ground level. The existence of the bank helped prevent the wall from being damaged by battering rams. Norman and Reader had to learn to detect the slightest traces of this bank in their section drawings.

The line of the Roman wall
This program of detective work was tedious and difficult, since the observers had to travel along the 5-kilometer course of the wall from the Tower of London to Blackfriars looking for opportunities to dig. Sometimes they had to wait several years before a certain length was exposed. There is a Roman bastion beneath the Wardrobe Tower of the fortifications of the Norman Keep of the Tower of London. From there the wall was followed to Fenchurch Street, where it curved westward.

At Bevis Marks and Camomile Street—where Bastion No. 10, as it came to be labeled, had been found in 1876—the wall was also found. In the modern street called London Wall, as one might guess, the modern road is on the course of the Roman defense. It was not until World War II and the excavations that were carried out afterward that the fort at Cripplegate was found at Bastion No. 12. There the Roman foundations took a sudden turn to the south parallel to Noble Street. From there the observers decided that the wall turned at Aldersgate, and under Newgate Prison a massive Roman gateway was found. The famous old prison was demolished, and the foundations were fully exposed and plans drawn.

All this patient collecting of plans and drawings gave the people of the time a possible plan of the town. It did not explain why there were those curious sharp turns at the Cripplegate bastion and again at Aldersgate. One archaeologist, Dr. Mortimer Wheeler, who helped collect all the existing evidence about Roman London in 1929 and put it in a book, did suggest that there might have been a fort there for a short time. Proof of this was not found until the 1950's.

30

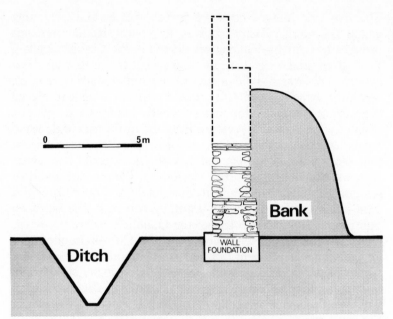

Section to show
city defenses
with wall
construction,
outer ditch, wall
and bank behind
wall.

0 — 5 m

Bank

WALL
FOUNDATION

Ditch

This story shows how patient archaeologists have to be. They can try to suggest reasons for the things they find, but they have to be very careful not to go further and invent reasons. After merely noting these curious sharp turns of the wall, archaeologists has to wait patiently for more large-scale operations to be possible before speculating further on the reasons for them.

OBSERVERS OF EXCAVATIONS IN
LATER WORKS IN THE CITY OF LONDON

The 1928 book containing all the information collected about Roman London has been the work of a group of people called the Royal Commission for Historical Monuments. They publish complete lists of ancient remains in each county in England, Scotland, Wales, and Northern Ireland. Their work is never finished as evidence is always being discovered. The commission consists of archaeologists, architects, and other specialists who work as a team.

It was in the 1920's that the Society of Antiquaries of London appointed the first Inspector of London Excavations. 31

This was Eric Birley who was later followed by G. C. Dunning and F. Cotteril. Their job was to record Roman remains brought to light by building operations in the City of London. F. Cotteril added much to the knowledge of the Roman street system. This was a difficult task since Roman roads were made of hard-rammed gravel and given a cementlike appearance on the surface partly by the engineers who made the streets and partly by the constant pressure from the traffic that had passed over them. In general, so little of the road surface had survived that often little more than patches of gravel could be plotted. By carefully noting the exact position of the patches and their relation to one another and to the buildings, Cotteril provided vital information from which a grid system of streets was later built up by Ralph Merrifield of the Guildhall Museum.

Another observer who worked in the City of London was G. C. Dunning. He went out and noted foundations and added to the plans already known. He also found many stretches of foundation that helped fill in the details of the basilica at Leadenhall. He also made valuable maps. These maps showed where burned pottery had been found. All this pottery was of the same date, and by putting dots on a map to show where the sherds or fragments were found, it was possible to see how far the fire of Boudicca (and also other fires) had spread. Archaeologists call these maps distribution maps. They are another form of keeping a record. Cards, books, squared paper are the kinds of records that field officers, who keep an eye on workmen's trenches, take with them. They put down what they see and what they measure. This is how both Cottrell and Dunning worked among the buildings in London.

The greatest opportunity for exploration came after World War II when a special committee to supervise the work was formed. For the first time a planned program of excavation was possible. But it must not be forgotten that the policy of this committee was based on what had been found out about London by the observers of the nineteenth century and later.

Sir Christopher Wren, when he built St. Paul's Cathedral, knew nothing of the line of the Roman town wall. He did not have the time or opportunity to think of what he knew of Roman towns or their walls. This knowledge might have helped the scholars of the seventeenth century to record finds.

32   Today archaeologists spend a great deal of time reading past

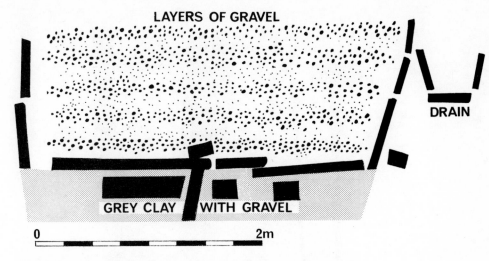

LAYERS OF GRAVEL

DRAIN

GREY CLAY **WITH GRAVEL**

0   2m

Section through a Roman road showing layers of gravel. Based on a section near Bucklersbury House.

records before they put a spade in the ground. Any piece of information about a site is considered; it is a clue that might lead to some piece of deduction when trenches are opened.

The next step is to go to the site and to walk around it with old plans. These may be inaccurate, but they show what was known about the site. Some feature that may have been missed before is noted. Sometimes the fact that modern streets run in certain directions may indicate ancient lines of defenses. This has happened in London. Such outdoor activity without excavation is called field work. Sometimes it enables an archaeologist to suggest a theory that he proves or disproves afterward by digging.

It is important to remember all these steps before we read about the excavations in London after World War II. It might be thought that with all this scientific planning and reasoning before the trenches are dug the excitement is lost. But in reading about the problems and activities during the last 20 years in London there were many remarkable finds and wonderful discoveries.

MODERN EXCAVATION IN LONDON

After the 1939–45 war the large areas of London damaged by   33

Selection of smith's tools from the Walbrook and Bank of England site. The hammer on the right may be from the post-mediaeval period.

bombing gave a further chance for excavation. An administrative body, called the Roman and Medieval London Excavation Council, was set up to organize the operation. Professor W. F. Grimes, then director of the London Museum, was appointed to direct the work. All excavations have some kind of administrative or governing body to direct the complex administration of the operation and to receive financial grants made for the project.

The problems which confronted these excavations in London were not easy to overcome. Buildings had been demolished, but there were concrete floors and tiled basements that had to be hacked through before Roman levels could be reached. Their removal often took a long time. Also, trenches could be dug to explore historical problems only when contractors made it possible and time was allowed.

It was not only Roman levels that had to be excavated. Several historical periods had to be considered at the same time.

34   Roman problems are our concern, but the remains left by the

Saxons are also of great importance. The development of medieval London and the city churches also had to be probed.

Many times the excavators were to find that the previous developments, whether office buildings, sewers, or public services, had already irreparably damaged the remains of earlier periods. The final frustration was to find that as the natural land surface of the Roman period rose higher toward the north, the modern disturbances had swept them away completely.

Sometimes while Professor Grimes and his team were patiently continuing their task, sudden emergencies would occur. Impatient developers constructed modern buildings at a much more rapid pace than any previous rebuilders in the history of London.

The staff of the Guildhall Museum was active in dangerous rescue operations during the early 1950's in the Walbrook area. The deep concrete piers of the modern buildings were thrust down into the mud of the old riverbed. This allowed a tremendous range of objects to be salvaged; because of the damp conditions, leather and timber, both materials that do not normally survive, did emerge almost unscathed from this area.

Below: iron trenching tool from the Walbrook on the site of Bucklersbury House.

PUBLIC INTEREST IN EXCAVATION

During the years since the end of World War II, there has been an intensive rise in the interest of ordinary people in the work of excavation. The accounts and pictures of the buildings and finds published in papers and journals, the vivid reports and explanations given on radio and television have been the main causes of the interest.

Several societies and groups have been formed from time to time to help in the work of rescuing, excavating, and study. One such group was the Thames Basin Observers Group, which, as its name implied, ranged over a wide area long the banks of the Thames, salvaging objects of every period, not only Roman. For many years the young members, galvanized into action by their leaders, worked either by exploring the mud and gravel deposits of the banks of the river or by digging quickly to clarify a problem before bulldozers moved in.

Since the war, while Professor Grimes and his trained assistants were working on the most detailed and complicated trenches, a band of volunteers gradually got together to work at weekends on certain sections that were laborious and that 35 helped the main work. Ever since, a group has always remained to carry out emergency excavations from time to time as the staff of the Guildhall Museum requires help. Today this society is called the City of London Archaeological Society. The results of its current activity are often to be found on display at the museum. Some recent work which it has done was to carry out further exploration on the site of the basilica and forum. The full-time field officer on the staff of the London Museum also has a group of helpers on whom he can call for emergency help.

The Southwark and Lambeth Archaeological Society works intensively in the important area south of the Thames, where little was known until a very short time ago. Modern development around the section known as the Elephant and Castle has given scope for discoveries.

Within the framework of the London and Middlesex Society there are many groups that have joint meetings and conferences. They extend their influences to the outskirts of London, since finds in the country around London are equally important. From these areas the food and leather and other raw materials arrived for London's inhabitants.

Today deliberate planning is causing old buildings to be pulled down to be replaced by tall modern buildings with deep concrete piles as foundations. Foundations for skyscrapers have to go down deeper into the earth than foundations for shorter buildings. It has always been an established fact in archaeology that no one can reexcavate an area once worked upon. Layers are destroyed when they are cleared and the finds all taken out. In laying these deep modern foundations, medieval remains are bulldozed away, and no further excavation will ever be possible.

This is why careful observation is even more vital now than it ever was.

CHAPTER TWO

The Excavation of the Temple of Mithras

In the rescue operations carried out during the last century, it was very much a question of luck whether much information about where finds came from was noted down. Occasionally measurements of the position of a find in relation to the modern pavement was obtained, but few notes were made on whether the finds were in a pit or above a floor. The color of the surrounding earth was rarely noted. All these details are routine observations today.

Nowadays excavations, although often still carried out as rescue operations under great difficulty, are undertaken to answer certain questions about a site. Part of the basic training of a modern archaeologist is that he must think as he works. In finding out one answer to a problem, he invariably finds more puzzles, which is the ever fascinating part of excavation. When it is remembered that it was only in 1876 that workmen were first employed to dig in order to find out the full dimensions of a bastion, it shows how recently our methods have evolved.

In the 1930's, when observers were first employed to collect information about the Roman town plan, they were determined to find out where the streets of the Roman town lay. As we have seen, the Romans always used a grid system of streets, so that when a few street foundations were observed, the grid could be completed, at least for one period, and the buildings plotted on it. *Street system*

As in all excavations, the preparatory field work had first to be carried out for this. Professor Grimes, when he became Director of the Roman and Medieval Excavation Council, adopted the same approach. He read all the accounts of the previous excavations that were available. He looked at all plans, sections, even the early ones, which were very brief. Before laying out his first trench, he read the detailed survey of Roman London which had been compiled and published in 1928 by the 37

Roman wooden piles on the site of Bucklersbury House, Walbrook.

Royal Commission for Historical Monuments. He noted the
outstanding problems, which included the fact that nothing was
known about the pre-Roman occupation of the site of London
and that a few timber buildings of uncertain date had been
found in the foreshore of the river at Brentford. It had never
been established whether these were remains of Iron Age huts
or whether they were foundations of an early Roman bridge.
Would there be a chance of finding any evidence that there had
been pre-Roman inhabitants in the area of London Bridge, or
would the evidence come from within the area of the City? In
clearing away buildings near the old bed of the Walbrook, there
might be an opportunity of seeing more of the timber buildings
found by Colonel Lane-Fox in the 1860's.

Another aim was to find out something of the extent of the
early Roman settlement of Londinium. Since written sources
had provided an account of the destruction of the settlement by
Boudicca, a strict search for a thick burned layer might lead to a
detection of some of these early levels. Trenches are dug to
reveal the plan of a building; this means that the two essential
aspects of archaeological recording can be carried out at the
same time and most effectively—namely, the horizontal plan of
the building and the vertical section of the levels.

The horizontal plan is the easiest to understand and plot out. *Technique*
The director of an excavation lays out artificially square
trenches whenever he can, leaving about 1 meter of soil between
them; this allows artificial "balks," or barriers, to remain. Sometimes there is no room to set out this "grid system" where the
trenches must be absolutely square. In that case the director
makes several rectangular trenches, which are much more
difficult to survey. The best method employs square trenches.
In this scheme the director will use small wooden pegs 5 centimeters square, each with a nail at the top in its very center.
These will be set out at the corners of the squares, perhaps 3.75
meters, 3.25 meters, or 2 meters square. Each square is meti-
culously measured from the very center of these pegs—that is,
from the nail. To allow for the "balk" and the crossing at each
corner of the grid, 0.5 meter is allowed from each peg. This
allows a 3.75 square grid to have a 3.25 meter square trench.
Diggers can then walk along these artificial paths between
the squares. They can push their wheelbarrows along them,
though great care has to be taken not to knock the wooden pegs

at the corners of the grid out of their carefully measured positions.

The pegs are painted white, and the letter and numbers of each square are painted on them in clear black paint. The pegs are set diagonally to the squares so that it is clear what any one square is called—A I, A II, in one row next to B I, etc., and C I, etc. The necessity for this is clear when records are kept and when surveying is carried out from the pegs nearest the square.

Survey in buildings   To survey any feature—a column base, hearth, or an especially important find in a square—the recorder and his assistants will use two steel measuring tapes. The assistants will fix their thumbs firmly on the end of the tapes on the nails on top of two of the most convenient pegs; the recorder will hold the other two ends and measure the distance from each peg. He will write down each measurement and the numbers of the pegs from which they were taken. If he is recording a large irregular feature, he will take several measurements, and later, in the drawing office, he will take his compass and ruler, and with the point of the compass on the point to represent the nails, he will measure off these distances and draw an arc. Where the two intersect, he will have an accurately plotted point on his plan. This is called triangulation and is the simplest form of surveying for features found within the squares of an area dug. The surveyor who deals with the planning of the whole complex building has to take much more complicated measurements from a fixed datum line. This is a line related to a permanent feature near a site that is marked on the Ordnance Survey map of the area, so that the whole of the newly discovered building can be related to a permanent feature. It is most important to do this since the exact position of the building must be known even after all traces of it have been destroyed by excavation and rebuilding. Very occasionally a building is covered over by a field surface and farmers resume working above it. But should it be necessary to uncover that building at a future date, it could quickly be found by reference to the record on the map.

Another mark to which the director of an excavation has to relate it is called a bench mark; this is a sign 𝍖 found on certain buildings and it records the height above sea level of that particular point. This is a measurement surveyed and fixed by the Ordnance Survey Department, and these bench marks are found in every part of the country. Why is it important to relate

Relief of the god Mithras killing the bull found near the site of the temple in 1889.

ancient buildings to this fixed point on vertical heights? Because it is most necessary to relate a building in height or level to another. In a town like London this is of the greatest importance, as levels are one above the other in such a densely packed sequence.

One part of London made available to Professor Grimes for exploration was the ground where office buildings put up in 1889 stood near Bond Court. It was here that a relief sculpture of the god Mithras had been discovered in 1889. Fortunately the site was large enough for an area excavation, so the possibility of making complete plans of any foundations that might remain was good.

In spite of the large modern concrete cellars that had stood over the area that was available for exploration, the archaeologists put down larger trenches than they were normally able to mark out. A remarkably complete rectangular building emerged. It measured 17 meters long by 7 meters wide. It was set, or aligned, from west to east. The entrance was at the eastern end; the step of the threshold was found with pivot holes in position 41 on either side. The iron collars from the pivot posts of the doors were still in position, although the wooden posts had rotted away. At the other end of the building was a curve, or apse, outside and a niche inside. In addition to the large curve, the builders had added a rounded buttress on each side so that the outside had three curves.

Uncovering the plan   Inside, the building had been divided into three zones by two sleeper foundations—that is, two parallel foundations laid to floor level only, but planned to strengthen the building and to take the weight of the columns set at intervals along their line in order to support the roof of the two side aisles. Finding a foundation is not easy during an excavation. The ruined wall has usually collapsed into a spread on either side of the core of the part of the wall that survives. Sometimes the upper part of the wall has been robbed in a post-Roman period, and only the foundations of the walls survive. In this building the masonry had survived, together with many traces of the timber fittings that had been put into it. The damp conditions caused these to survive.

Indications survived of the floors of the structure, which were of laid wooden boards. In all, eight floors were detected lying one above the other. Each one had to be carefully uncovered and the finds made on each kept separately and labeled. The floor of the apse, or niche, had originally been nearly one meter above the floor of the nave. As new floors were laid in the nave, the difference of level became less, until at last there was no difference at all. The whole building was set 75 centimeters into the

Plan of the Temple of Mithras showing the position where the different sculptures were found.

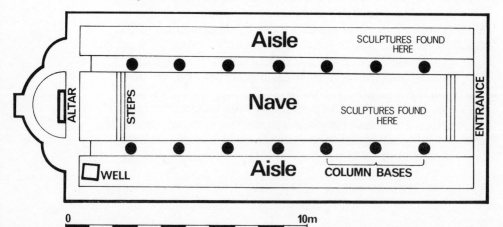

ground. Two steps led from the entrance on the east side down onto the floor of the nave.

The central aisle of the nave was 2.75 meters wide. On both sides, the platforms of the side aisles were raised higher than the floor of the central aisle. Traces of the upright timbers supporting the platforms were found in position. The bases of seven columns were found on either side of the nave. These supported the roof of the side aisles. It was clear from these clues that the building was a shrine. When a house is excavated, the range of coarse and good pottery, coins, and personal ornaments—the occupation material as it is called—is varied and found in great quantity. In this building chiefly ritual objects—vessels or utensils used by the officials or priests—were the only objects found. These were unusual and exotic. The plan of the building was that of a temple, not a house. The niche, or apse, at the western end was where the figure of a god or goddess would have been placed because of this niche, this plan is known as the basilican type.

A rectangular block set on the latest floor in front of the apse was clearly the plinth (or platform base) for a statue. The block was set on top of a coin of Constantine, emperor in the fourth century A.D. Was this a Christian shrine? There were no clues to identify the shrine as Christian in this, the last period of its use. In excavation it is always the same; the last building is on top, and the excavators have to proceed carefully from the last phase or chapter in the story to the lowest or earliest building.

A Christian shrine?

As work proceeded to strip off the seventh floor in the area north of the northern sleeper foundation and near the easternmost column bases, a mass of red tile lying above a pit was found. No digger should ever penetrate below the level that he is stripping at the time. The horizontal layers must be stripped systematically. A pit is one of the exceptions; this is regarded as a complication that must be cleared. The top edges of a pit must be noted in order to know for certain from which floor level it was dug. The red tiles were removed, and it was clear that this pit had been dug from the early-fourth-century floor of the temple. A marble head of the god Mithras and a fine marble head of the goddess Minerva were found lying in the pit. Clearly both had been deliberately buried in order to protect them from being damaged by Christians.

The shrine could be identified at last as a mithraeum, or 43

Marble head of the god Mithras
found in the temple in the Walbrook
area.

Mithras

temple of Mithras. The young god was wearing on his head the
characteristic cap always associated with Mithras. A separate
fragment of marble turned out to be the neck formerly attached
to the head. Since the marble had been buried for so many centuries near an iron deposit, it was disfigured by an iron encrusta-
tion. Sculptures or pots often break on being removed from the
soil, since pressure of heavy weights above them sometimes
causes fracture. After carefully cleaning away the soil and lifting it gently, this sculpture was safely raised and taken to the
laboratory of the British Museum to be cleaned. The head was
turned and appeared to strain away from something in front;
this is the characteristic pose of Mithras when plunging his
dagger into the neck of the bull. It was the main belief of the
followers of Mithras that he had killed the evil bull at the
44   request of the sun. Animals are shown drinking the blood of the

bull while the god, astride its shoulders, looks away. This is the same pose as shown on the relief found in 1889 in Bond Lane. During the cleaning of the head, damage and discoloration on the marble surface was found to contain carbon. This had certainly been caused by fumes from altar fires rising up toward this main sculptured relief of the god set in the niche above the apse.

The head of the goddess Minerva was also an elegant portrait. *Minerva* A plain band passed over the hair on the brow. The crown of the head was flat and rough because a marble helmet would have been carved and set above it. Just as there are statues of various saints in a cathedral, several gods and goddesses are found in temples of the pagan period. The goddess of wisdom and war, Minerva, is often associated with Mithras.

Below the floor of the nave another group of sculptures was *Serapis* found. A large carved stone dish or bowl originally made to hold water was found upturned with an amazing collection of figures. These included a head of the god Serapis, an Egyptian deity with flowing locks and characteristic headdress. He was the god of fertility and afterlife. A very large hand—far bigger in scale than the head of Mithras—was also found. This held the pommel of a dagger; obviously this was the hand of the god plunging the dagger into the bull, but because of its size it must have belonged to another relief showing the god Mithras killing the bull. This brings the number of these sculptures, all of different sizes, found in London to three. Because of the large size of this hand there must be a larger mithraeum yet to be found. Did the worshipers rescue this hand from the larger shrine and bury it in the smaller one for safety?

Another delightful figurine, preserved in remarkable condi- *Mercury with* tion, was that of the god Mercury, seated, with a tortoise and *tortoise and* ram at his feet. Again, this god was associated with the cult of *ram* Mithras. The tortoise was a reminder that the god had invented the lyre by using its shell.

In a concealed cavity in the wall of the later mithraeum a small circular silver casket, with a lid, had been hidden. This was embossed with an elaborate mythological scene. Beneath the lid was a strainer. Obviously this had been used in the ritual of the cult. In design and workmanship this resembled the style fashionable in the Danube region. Some of the sculptures also showed foreign influences and were certainly not made in Britain. 45

Treasure trove　The excavation of the casket raised the question of treasure trove. Since the casket was of silver, it had to be brought to a special court. This declared it to be treasure trove—that is, the property of the Queen—since the original owners had deliberately buried it but had not recovered it. All objects of gold and silver found must be examined and considered in this way to see if they are treasure trove. Among the special privileges of the City of London is one that allows it to keep all treasures found within its boundaries. Because of this, the silver casket now belongs to the City and is on view at the Guildhall Museum.

Seldom do archaeologists find so many artistic and valuable objects when they are excavating a site. The rewards are usually much more humble, such as sherds of pottery and fragments of bronze. It was fortunate that it was possible to excavate carefully the greater part of the shrine, though not of the vestibule or entrance hall.

It was not possible to leave exposed the foundations of the Temple of Mithras so that visitors could view them in the same position as they were found. A very large building was destined to stand there. The owners of this structure, Bucklersbury House, very kindly paid for lifting the foundations and relaying them on a terrace outside Temple Court so that people could later see the shrine. It is now on a raised platform, but visitors must remember that originally it was set into the ground.

CHAPTER THREE

What Do Finds from Excavations Reveal About the History of Londinium?

Now that the way in which archaeologists work has been described, what have the finds from the Roman levels revealed about the early history of Londinium? Two important questions that students of any Roman town ask are: Where did the local inhabitants live before the Romans came? How big was the first settlement?

To answer the first question, archaeologists must see if there *Iron Age* are timber houses with pre-Roman pottery on their floors under *discoveries* the early Roman levels. The search begins by looking at all the records to see if any of the timber buildings which have been found could have had black or gray Iron Age pottery associated with them. It is different from Roman pottery. It is softer and is shaped into storage jars, plates, beakers, and bowls unlike those of the Romans. Sometimes the bowls and plates were well made, elaborate shapes thrown on a potter's wheel. Often they were made by hand and were simply useful storage jars with rough grooves made by a wooden comb on the surface. But none of this pottery has ever been found with the timber buildings in the area of Roman occupation at Londinium.

The only proved pre-Roman huts that have been found are those at Battersea and Mortlake, both well away from the City. The timbers once thought to have been pre-Roman along the riverside in other areas are now thought to be some of the earliest Roman structures—perhaps wharf buildings.

When the landing strips of Heathrow Airport, now London *Timber shrine* Airport, were being laid out in a tremendous rush during the *at Heathrow* difficult days of World War II, a timber building was found. This consisted of two squares in the ground. The timber foundations of the outer square may have supported the columns of a veranda while the inner square was the actual wall of a temple. Archaeologists who saw it were thrilled because this was the first time they had seen this plan of a temple in timber. Previously all 47 examples had been built of masonry and had been Roman, but the Heathrow temple was associated with Iron Age pottery. It meant that this type of building was in use in Britain before the Romans arrived. Later temples of this plan were built, but always in stone.

The picture that we have of the London area before the Romans came is of a number of scattered native communities. We know that Celts were living close to London at Heathrow, at Brentford, and at Caesar's Camp, Wimbledon Common. So far we have found no native building, not even a cluster of huts, on the site of the Roman town.

WAS THERE A ROMAN TRADING POST ON THE SITE OF LONDINIUM?

Up to the present we have no definite knowledge of a native settlement very close to the Roman town. But what is the earliest building on the site of the Roman settlement itself? Could there have been a small trading post, perhaps during the period between Julius Caesar's expeditions in 55–54 B.C. and the invasion of the Emperor Claudius A.D. 43? Caesar crossed the Thames river during his second campaign and imposed a tribute on the tribes he conquered before he was recalled to Gaul.

Other Roman writers describe the bravery of traders who often risked their lives to establish trading posts in countries which had not been taken over by the Roman government, such as the area beyond the Rhine among the tribes in unconquered Germany. Traders supervised cargoes in ships and by overland transport. Roman pottery has been found as far afield as India. A ship with a cargo full of pottery was found wrecked in the Thames estuary near Pudding Pan Rocks.

In recent centuries we know of traders who went to Canada, China, India, and other countries to establish trading posts and later to found colonies. We know about these exploits because people wrote diaries and books about these expeditions. How can we prove the existence of early Roman traders? The Romans themselves did not write much about the activities of traders. The answer is pieced together by the discovery of objects.

Potters working in factories at Arretium in Italy toward the end of the first century B.C. and in the early part of the first century A.D. produced a range of very elegant dishes, drinking cups, *Pottery* platters, and bowls. These were pale pink, thin-walled, and of a fine fabric. As this pottery is found in many places from the native huts at the Sheepen site at Camulodunum (Colchester) in England to Mohenjo Daro in India, it shows the wide scale of Roman trade at that date.

Archaeologists always have to be careful to note the exact findspot of the Arretine ware. To prove trade before conquest, it has to be found with the black and gray pottery in occupation levels—that is, on floors with the debris of daily life. Unfortunately the sherds of Arretine found in the lowest levels in London have not been discovered within this setting. Therefore, it could be that they merely prove the early trade which happened after the invasion of A.D. 43, and it cannot be said definitely that the sherds were brought in before that date.

The timber huts of the traders have not been found, and so we must hope that we shall learn more one day of this phase of the town's history. But we might still imagine a few ships bringing in traders with this distinctive pottery and selling a few bowls, platters, or cups to the scattered groups of natives in the Thames Valley, even if they were not concentrated in one particular spot that became Londinium.

THE FIRST GREAT DISASTER TO THE TOWN

Have you seen a shed burning? Often, in spite of efforts to save *Destruction by* it, a timber building will burn fiercely and in no time at all a *fire* black and white powdery smoking patch is all that is left where the shed stood. Not all the timber has become black powder. Some of it survives in charred lumps and fragments. But the white ash covers everything and is blown about by the wind. Nails lie among the black mass; glass, if the building had a window, is a hardened mass of melted substance. The foundations of the shed still lie in the ground. The rain consolidates the whole area of burning, so that in time it becomes a thick layer of black earth, which is gradually covered over with unburned soil.

Imagine a tremendous fire happening in the rectangular timber warehouses, houses, and shops of the first settlements at Londinium, Camulodunum, and Verulamium. These timber buildings had, in addition to the main oak beams of the framework, panels of interwoven strips of oak which were plastered 49 with clay. When this was burned, it turned red; it is called daub. Therefore, in all burned levels in the Roman period the black remains of the timber are mixed with lumps of red daub. The burnt level would be 24 to 30 centimeters deep because the buildings were quite large and sometimes high with a loft above the first floor. The corners of the buildings were heavy square or rectangular timbers that had been cut out of large tree trunks. The smaller roof timbers would have crashed down on top of shelves with pottery on them, on floors with furniture, on wine jars standing in corners, and on all the objects normally found in the houses. In Londinium, Camulodunum, and Verulamium archaeologists dug down deeply in trenches and found a thick burnt layer, for which they had to find both a date and a cause. For these thick black layers were not a local fire in one house, as they were found in trenches dug in many places in all three Roman towns. Such fires could have been caused only by a major disaster to the area.

Revolt of the Iceni under Boudicca The Roman writer Tacitus has described how, in A.D. 61, while the governor of the province (who was also commander of the army) was campaigning in north Wales against unconquered tribes there, the Iceni and Trinovantes of East Anglia and Essex collected together under the leadership of Boudicca, the widowed queen of the Iceni. First they completely destroyed the Roman settlement at Camulodunum. Though Suetonius Paulinus, the commander, hurried back, he did not have enough troops to meet the angry natives before they attacked Londinium and Verulamium. Paulinus did not receive reinforcements from the Second Legion in the west in time to save them. So he abandoned these towns to their fate and waited until he could meet the native army at a site where he had the maximum advantage and where he knew he could conquer them.

Meanwhile, Boudicca's tribe, angry at the treatment given to the family of their ruler, and the unreasonable demands of the Roman moneylenders who had called for repayment with extortionate rates, joined the natives of Essex whose land had been taken from them by the government to be given to new citizens of Camulodunum. Together they vented their feeling by burning and killing.

In Londinium one dramatic find in a trench under St. Swithin's House, Walbrook, showed the confusion that occurred at that time. It consisted of a pit in which lay the usual rubbish

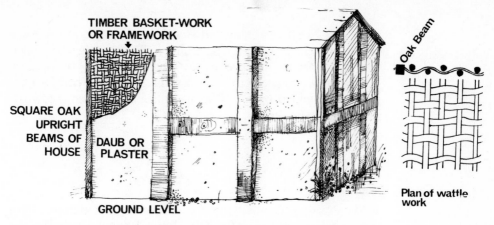

TIMBER BASKET-WORK
OR FRAMEWORK

SQUARE OAK
UPRIGHT
BEAMS OF
HOUSE

DAUB OR
PLASTER

GROUND LEVEL

Oak Beam

Plan of wattle work

Reconstruction of a wooden house with "wattle and daub" construction.

that was thrown out of the house: broken pottery, animal bones, the remains of a meal, and some rotten vegetables which had turned black and decayed. On top of this a large amphora, or wine jar, was found lying beside a smaller two-handled jar. Both were almost complete—only one break in the neck of the wine jar. This suggested that the contents had been hastily drunk and the two vessels cast aside. On top of these was the clear filling of the Boudiccan fire. Did the last inhabitants of a nearby house drink the wine before they left, or did the attackers loot the cellar and then toss the jars into the pit?

Evidence of panic during attack

It is such small pieces of evidence that are used to prove the catastrophic destruction of the town. The burned daub and timbers have been noted in many areas where trenches have been cut down. The timbers are from the framework of the houses, and the daub is the clay which was plastered onto the panels of more pliable timber supported by the vertical upright beams of the houses and the sleeper or horizontal beams of the foundations. From the discovery of such fragments we know that the earliest settlement at Londinium was on the hill to the east of the Walbrook stream. On a modern street map this is the area between Cannon Street and Cornhill extending eastward toward Gracechurch Street.

The half-filled rubbish pit under St. Swithin's House stood in the middle of the Walbrook Valley. It seems that a number of buildings stood near a bridge which had spanned the stream there. A few buildings stood on the western side. However, at   51 present it is not possible to give a definite outline to the early settlement which was the first London. Tacitus suggests that it was not defended by a bank or ditch. This may be because houses were being erected between the late 40's when Londinium was founded by the Romans and A.D. 61 when the settlement was destroyed.

EVIDENCE FROM THE DISTRIBUTION
MAPS OF SAMIAN POTTERY

It has already been noted that G. C. Dunning began to plot onto maps of London the findspots of burned Samian pottery. The names "Samian" and "terra sigillata" have been given to a special type of Roman pottery. Because it was thought at first that this came from the Mediterranean island of Samos, the name "Samian" was given to the ware. This was later found to be wrong, as this pottery was produced in kilns in France. So the name "terra sigillata" was given to it because it described the molded designs on the surface of the bright red ware. The name "Samian" is still used sometimes because it is shorter, but it

Bowl of Samian pottery showing relief decoration. (Form Dragendorff 29.) Found in a refuse pit in King William St.

must be remembered that the pottery found in Britain was made in France.

Scholars studied the different shapes of this pottery and found that these changed from time to time as people tired of well-known shapes. They also found that the potters stamped the plates and dishes with their names and that designers also stamped their names among the patterns when the bowls were decorated. Using these stamps and the dates obtained when vessels of different shapes were found with different coins, archaeologists have written books giving dates to each type of Samian pot and plate. Today, when a piece of Samian ware is found, archaeologists can use it to date the building level in which it lies, and any coarse pottery, brooches, or other items found with the piece of Samian.

It was because Samian pottery is so useful for dating that G. C. Dunning worked away, plotting the findspot of each fragment of burned and blackened Samian ware on his distribution map. From the shape of Samian pots he found that it was not just pottery of Boudicca's time that showed signs of burning. There must have been another big fire in the reign of Hadrian (A.D. 117–132) since some Samian of that date also showed signs of burning. So two maps were made to show the extent of each fire.

We know of no historical event that could have caused the second fire, which seems to have covered an area of 10 hectares, but a growing settlement built mainly of timber may have been accidentally set on fire. Although Roman towns had some kind of fire department—people who came with buckets and a water-cart to the scene of a fire to try to put it out—they would be no match for a really fierce blaze which would quickly spread. The Great Fire of London in 1666 was a similar disaster.

The flourishing Roman London that was rebuilt in the late first century A.D. after Boudicca's fire was again mainly concentrated on the hill east of the Walbrook. Some buildings were found on the west of the stream, but these were not tightly packed together. Although many finds have been revealed in the area north of Walbrook, it is more difficult to make sure that these were from buildings, since they could have come from boats on the river and stalls in a busy market on its banks. There may not have been any houses in this area.

Finger ring marked with the word "AMICA" and decorated with bearded head, from the area of the Walbrook stream.

Dating

53

Street plan At no time has there been evidence that the Roman government ever allowed haphazard building of houses and shops in any of its towns. Archaeologists know that a fully grown Roman town plan had a chessboard arrangement of streets (see page 15). The streets were laid out in a grid at right angles to each other, with square blocks of buildings in the spaces. Each block was called an insula, or island, by the Romans. Modern archaeologists, who also use the same word, number these insulae as they are discovered; this is a useful way of recording the different buildings in them and listing the finds in that particular block.

Another question when considering the origin of towns is: when did it have a regular grid system of streets? Sometimes buildings are found to be not quite in a straight line with one another as they should be if they all fronted along the same street. This might mean that the governing body of the town had altered the plan of the streets in that town because of some special development. Perhaps a road became important, and it was necessary to include buildings near it within the wall of the settlement at a date later than that of the original foundation.

North of a line along Lombard Street in London there have been found the foundations of a building which, from the finds it contained, appears to have been there from the period before the fire of Boudicca and her followers. The gravel running from east to west along the front of this building was a street, and must have been one of the first roads in Londinium. It continued in use throughout the Roman period. Lombard Street, which follows the line of this Roman road, can claim to be the oldest road in London.

Ragstone The discovery of this early building and roadway also proves *foundations* that there were tidy blocks of buildings in the first Londinium. Some of them were important enough to have ragstone foundations even when they had a timber framework for the top of the walls and for the roof. Since the majority of the buildings were constructed completely of timber, one particularly large building standing north of the line of Lombard Street with ragstone foundations and dated to the first century A.D. might well have been used for official business. The cost of ragstone foundations at such an early date would have been considerable. This building

54 might have been the residence of the governor of the province or

another official, or it might have been the office where the taxes of the province were collected or even the building which housed one of the branches of the imperial post.

Enough is known of the Roman system of government to make these suggestions possible explanations. Just as Roman town planners insisted that all who came to live in towns built their homes or shops within the regular grid system of streets, so taxes had to be paid both to the local authority and to the central provincial government. Since Londinium stood at one end of an important bridge, it is possible that those crossing the bridge had to pay a toll or some local charge. It is also possible that ships paid a tax when unloading their cargo at the wharves.

Since few foundations of buildings of the first century A.D. have been found near the wharves, and buildings of later times are not always complete, what other evidence can be used to show what an important place Londinium became in commercial and government affairs?

INSCRIPTIONS AS EVIDENCE OF
COMMERCIAL AND GOVERNMENT ACTIVITY

Archaeologists working in the Roman levels are more fortunate than those who excavate in pre-Roman sites in Britain. The Romans brought the knowledge of writing with them, and we are helped by some accounts, written in Latin, that have survived. Archaeologists working in Roman Britain are even more fortunate since, in addition to a few historical accounts, there is an account of the life of Agricola, one of the governors of the province, written by his son-in-law Tacitus. Another writer compiled biographies of the Emperors Claudius, Nero, and Hadrian. Names of governors of Britain are obtained from some of these writings. Thus, in several cases we know who was responsible for building a fort or replanning a town.

The prehistoric archaeologists can never do this since they find only buildings, enclosures, and burial places of people who lived here before writing was introduced. They can hardly ever know the names of those who built and used the sites.

The revolt of Boudicca and her followers, the Iceni, was mentioned by Tacitus, who describes the attack on Camulodunum, Verulamium, and Londinium. So, when archaeologists found the very thick layer of burning containing pottery and coins of the 55 mid-first century A.D., they knew that it was caused deliberately by the Britons and that it was no accidental fire.

Inscriptions　　Archaeologists are also often fortunate enough to find Latin inscriptions or lettering on stones. These were used in many places and for many purposes. On very large buildings a large stone giving the name of the emperor in whose reign the building was set up would be built into the wall in a prominent position. In addition, it would give the purpose of the building, e.g., marketplace (forum) or town hall (basilica), theater or temple. At the end of the inscription there would usually be added the names of the leading town councilors of the local authority where the building was situated. Just as foundation stones set in modern buildings have the name of the king or queen reigning at the time and sometimes also the name of the local mayor and aldermen who were in office when the foundation stone was laid.

Sometimes a single individual paid for the erection or repair of a building. These were more often public baths, temples, or theaters than civic buildings. The name of the benefactor would be added prominently at the end. In Londinium there would have been many such inscriptions. In the large forum under Leadenhall market no doubt repairs were carried out several times on the different parts of the building. Unfortunately no inscriptions have yet been found. But at Viroconium (Wroxeter) and Verulamium (St. Albans) inscriptions of the civic kind have been found. At Aquae Sulis (Bath) a citizen rebuilt a temple to Diana.

Lettering in　　Stonemasons were important Roman craftsmen who devel-
stone　　oped the beautiful style of incised lettering in stone for which the Romans have become famous. Their Latin on the stones gradually became a form of abbreviated language or shorthand. They used this language on many other kinds of stones. On tombstones, such as the one illustrated on page 62, the names of the dead man and the dead man's father, the country from which the dead man came, and his career were all set out. In the tomb inscription of Classicianus his wife's name was added.

Milestones were erected by the government. On each one were the name of the emperor in whose reign it was set up, then the names of the nearest towns and the distance between them.

In many places altars were set up to different gods or goddesses. On these square blocks of stone with curved tops, the dedication to the deity was incised, together with the name and

56　　career of the man who had caused it to be erected. Sometimes he

Roof-tile stamped with the official mark of the financial officer of the province in London, "*PP. BR. LON.*"

stated the reason for setting up the altar. Perhaps he had promised to do so if he returned safely from a journey or recovered from an illness.

Tiles found in 1868 on the site of Cannon Street Station had on them the letters *PP. BR. LON.* Sometimes the letters *P. P. BR.* are found with or without the letters *LON.* No one is sure what the first letter *P* stands for in the kind of shorthand which was devised to save space and labor. It could be that the first letter *P* stands for "Procurator." The rest is easy since it is known that *P. BR.* is "Provinciae Britanniae." It may be that this is the official stamp put on the tiles before they were baked to state that they had been made in the official kilns maintained by the financial officer of the provincial government. *LON* or *LOND* is the abbreviation for "Londinium." This tells us that this official was in charge of this particular tilemaking center. If the building in which the tiles had been used was an official one, it had clearly been supplied with tiles from the official kiln.

Official tiles

All tiles—there were various shapes used in different parts of a Roman building—are always washed carefully when they are found in an excavation. They often show a variety of marks. All are grooved by wooden combs or by the fingertips of the tile maker. This is a method of making them adhere more firmly to

57

Lead sheet with cursive Latin curse written on it, found in Prince's Street.

Early graffiti

the cement that fixed them in position. On some the footprints of animals—dogs, goats, or hens—are noted. These domesticated animals walked over the wet tile before it had been baked.

But the most exciting scratches on the surface of a tile may be the handwriting of the maker or his companion. These scribblings of the Romans scratched on tiles or on metal are called graffiti. On a tile from Warwick Lane the following sentence had been scratched with a stick: "AUSTALIS DIBUS XIII VAGATUR SIB COTIDIM." ("Austalis has been wandering off on his own every day for the last fortnight.") This brief sentence gives rise to much speculation about possible reasons for this solitary walk!

From Prince's Street, London, a sheet of lead was found with the following writing on it: "T[ITUS] EGNATIUS TYRANUS DEFICTUS EST ET PUBLIUS CICEREIUS FELIX DEFICTUS EST." ("Titus Egnatius Tyranus is hereby solemnly cursed; likewise Publius Cicereius Felix.") This is a curse, and such inscriptions are often found in sacred shrines. Several are known from other Roman sites. An individual from whom something had been stolen or who had suffered some misfortune would go to the priest of a temple and ask him to write

58

out a curse and nail it up in the temple for all to see. Perhaps money was paid to the temple funds. The individual would then go away feeling that his favorite god or goddess would curse the culprits for their wrongdoing.

Wooden tablets have often been found during excavations in Londinium, especially from the damp levels of the Walbrook. The commonest type of memorandum notebook known to the Romans consisted of two rectangular pieces of wood folded together. The inside pages, as it were, were recessed to receive wax. The writer used a bronze stylus, an instrument pointed at one end and flat at the other, to write on the wax. When it was no longer needéd, the wax could be smoothed with the end of the stylus. Another message could then be written on the wax. Sometimes the writer pressed so hard on the stylus that the point left marks on the wooden backing, and we can read writing that would otherwise have vanished with the wax. On the wood of a tablet found in the Walbrook on the site of the Bank of England were these letters: "PROC AUG DEDERUNT BRIT PROV." This is translated as "issued by the Imperial Procurators of the Province of Britain." All property of a government department

Wooden "notebooks"

Wooden writing tablet and iron "stili" or instrument for writing on the wax which would have been in the recessed part of the tablet. Found on the site of the Bank of England.

would be stamped with such a mark. There were many sections of the Roman government. Judges conducted different types of trials. Town councilors dealt with various aspects of city life. One section of government dealt with the upkeep of streets and buildings, another with the conduct of markets and the taxes to be paid by merchants. All the government officials would work in buildings near the markets and in the center of the town. The imperial post was a network of messengers who traveled throughout the Empire carrying messages and dispatches on behalf of the emperor and provincial governor. They were servants of the imperial government, not of the local authority. In Londinium they would have had a separate building and no doubt an inscription to announce their function.

From inscriptions we have discovered that Londinium was not at first the capital of Roman Britain. Roman historians recorded that when the Emperor Claudius was at Camulodunum (Colchester) after his victory near the Thames, he decreed that the capital of the new province was to be the new city there. A temple was set up in the new town, which was to become a center where retired soldiers would live after they had left the army. One of the grievances which caused the local inhabitants to join with the Iceni in A.D. 60 was the rough treatment that they received when their land was taken by force for this reallocation.

However, there are indications that it was not long before the Roman government realized its mistake in so hastily announcing that Camulodunum was to be the capital. It was an awkward journey to Essex from the ports in Kent and from good routes for communications with the army. It is doubtful whether all the government offices ever went to Camulodunum, since the town was not completely built before the destruction of A.D. 60.

In the brief account of the revolt one Roman historian mentioned that Decianus Catus, the procurator, or chief financial officer, sent 200 men to help defend Camulodunum before it was attacked. He was in Londinium at the time and made his escape to the Continent before the revolt proceeded to Londinium. Does this mean that his office was already in that town?

One important inscription proves that the man who followed Decianus as procurator certainly lived and worked in Londinium. The story of its discovery and interpretation shows 60 what patience archaeologists need to have.

In 1852 when excavations were taking place in Trinity Place, *Tombstone of*
Tower Hill, one of the bastions (the semicircular solid projec- *Classicianus*
tions in front of the town wall) was uncovered. Built into the
solid part was a stone with a round scroll-like ornament lying
along the top on one side. This was the usual ornament for the
top of a tombstone or altar. The lettering read: "FAB[I].
ALPINI CLASSICIANI." This stood for the name "Fabius
Alpinus Classicianus." Certain scholars remembered that the
man who came to succeed Decianus was called Classicianus. He
had been described as a gentle man who did not approve of the
cruel policy of continued punishment that the Governor
Suetonius Paulinus inflicted on the natives after the defeat of
Boudicca and the tribesmen.

It was tempting to connect the inscription with this Classicianus. Some scholars were more cautious. They thought it
might only have been a coincidence, because there were many
people of this name. The full inscription was: "DIS MANIBUS
C. IUL. C. F. FAB. ALPINI CLASSICIANI."

Argument about this inscription continued without firm
evidence on either side until 1935. In that year an electricity
substation was being erected for London Transport on the
site of Bastion No. 2, where the first stone had been found.
This time the excavation went deeper, and another fragment
of the same inscription was found. This gave more information
about Classicianus: "PROC[URATOR]. PROVINC[IAE].
BRIT[ANNIAE]. IULIA. INDINFILIA. PACATA.
I[NDIANA]. UXOR." The translation of the whole inscription
is: "Sacred to the memory of C. Julius Alpinus Classicianus
of the Fabian tribe. . . . Procurator of the Province of Britain,
set up by his wife, Julia Pacata Indiana, daughter of Indus."
The parts in brackets were left out by the stonemasons as the
abbreviations they used would have been understood by the
people of the time. The second stone held the key to the problems of the first. It identified Classicianus as the procurator after
the Boudiccan revolt. The additional information about his wife,
Julia Pacata, daughter of Indus, gave another interesting glimpse
of the Roman civil service. Indus was a well-known cavalry officer
who had remained faithful to Roman authority in Gaul during
troubled times there similar to that following the Boudiccan revolt
in Britain. It shows how provincial people were given important
offices and how they respected tolerant and good government. 61

Tombstone of the Procurator Classicianus as restored in the British Museum.

A copy of this inscription is on display near the place where the pieces were found. The original stones are on view at the British Museum, set in a replica of the original tombstone.

This tombstone proves beyond doubt that the financial headquarters of Roman Britain was established in Londinium very soon after the disaster even if we cannot fully prove that it was there before. The tomb probably stood alongside one of the roads leading out of Londinium as was the custom in the Roman period. The bastion was not built until the third century. By that time some thrifty stonemason had brought along the stone in pieces for use in filling up the solid bastion. No member of the family would have survived 300 years later to protest. It might even have been the government which commanded all available stone for the defenses.

Remains of a very large building with massive walls were found when Cannon Street was being erected in 1868. This is now known as the "Governor's Palace" and may have been the offices of the procurator. Officially stamped tiles were found which suggest that this was a government building, and round a courtyard there were many small rooms that could have been offices. In another courtyard was a deep pool with fountains and drains which led to the early opinion that this was a municipal bath building.

THE BASILICA OR ADMINISTRATIVE HALL

Every Roman town had a distinctive building which consisted of a very large hall with rounded niches at one or both of the narrower ends. Normally the rectangular hall was so large that its roof had to be supported by two parallel rows of columns. There were platforms in the rounded niches where judges sat, for the basilica was the hall of justice where any lawsuit in the town was heard.

In most examples a row of small square offices was constructed on one side of this hall. There the clerks of the court and of the local authority would have had their offices. The assembly of local citizens who were elected as members of the ordo, or local council, would hold their meetings in the hall from time to time. Each year they elected two of their members to the leading positions in the council. They acted as chairmen of meetings and as chief executors of the regulations. Their position was similar to that of a mayor in modern local councils. But although this ordo could make regulations about local affairs, the emperor in Rome held the highest power. He alone decided the major issues. His orders and regulations arrived at every town by the messengers of the imperial post. The leading town councilors had to obey his command and make sure that all the local citizens knew of them.

If some of the small rooms off the main basilica were not being used by members of the local council, they were hired out of moneylenders or merchants. Merchants of different commodities formed a guild or an association, and these needed office accommodation. In a port such as Londinium there would be societies of corn merchants or timber merchants, for example.

In Londinium the building found under the medieval Leadenhall market has, as we have seen, been identified as the basilica. This hall with its massive parallel walls was built with the long sides from east to west; they measured 140 meters long. If this really is the basilica, then it is the largest example in the province. On further examination of the different foundations it was noticed that the earliest part of the foundations may only have been built 70 meters in length. Careful examination also showed that it was built after the Boudiccan revolt.

The western end appears to have been built about A.D. 80–90 because the floor of the northern aisle lay over pottery of that period. There were other unusual features about the basilica. It may have had two rows of offices on its northern side. This would have been needed by the active life of a port and a busy town.

Agricola's influence on building　　It seems that there was a considerable amount of rebuilding within the structure itself, as well as the resurfacing of streets around it. This rebuilding, between A.D. 79 and 85, took place when Gaius Julius Agricola was governor. The historian Tacitus, his son-in-law, wrote his biography, and while Tacitus described Agricola's achievements in conquering parts of the province, he also described what he did for the towns. Agricola encouraged the town councils to build imposing civic buildings, such as basilicas and baths. It could well be that in Londinium, which was by that time the most flourishing town in Britain, it was Agricola who inspired the local council to replan the central area and erect suitable administrative buildings.

In most of the towns of Britain the forum, or large open marketplace, lay to one side of the basilica. It consisted of a large rectangular space surrounded by a veranda. Under this covered walk, stood a row of small shops or booths. Merchants, guilds, or companies hired them out so that business could be transacted there.

There have been indications that such an open space or court stood on the south side of the London basilica. Traces of wall foundations that correspond to those on the western side have been seen in Gracechurch Street and in Lime Street Passage. These were in Castle Court, with an outer building in George Yard. However, the clearest traces of the forum were found in Gracechurch Street at the turning into Lombard Street. There a very elaborate fragment of what might have been the entrance to the south side was found. A coin of Hadrian was discovered in the yellow mortar of one of the column piers. This suggests that, although the scheme was planned in A.D. 80, the whole complex was not finished until the first quarter of the second century.

Evidence for building schemes at this time is found in other towns. At Viroconium (Wroxeter) public baths were planned in the late first century, but these were never completed. Years seem to have passed, and the solid foundations of the grand scheme were left unfinished. In the reign of the Emperor Hadrian the plan was adapted to that of a basilica and forum. A very large inscription gave the dedication of the new building to the reign of Hadrian. It might quite well have been the energetic Emperor Hadrian who ordered the government in Londinium to develop the marketplace to meet the needs of the growing town.

Excavations under the forum in this same area between Gracechurch Street and Lombard Street revealed an interesting deposit of layers. The ground into which the foundations of the forum had been dug was a mixed layer of sand, brick earth, and building debris. This suggests that before the builders laid out the forum, the plot of ground had to be deliberately filled in with mixed soil brought from elsewhere; this leveling of the ground often occurs in a town site. Occasionally building plots within an insula were left empty for a time, but the surrounding streets were constantly repaired so that the street level gradually rose. When the site was at last developed, rubble and debris had to be brought in to enable the foundations to be at the same level as the streets. Another reason might have been the need to make certain that the foundations were safe from flooding. In excavation the feel of the filling is easy to detect. It is not so hard and compressed as the natural soil. Another method of recognizing a deliberate filling of this kind is to study the finds. The objects found will be of many different dates. The pottery and coins might cover the whole period since the first landing of the Romans in the middle of the first century A.D.

How coins help to date a building
A layer can have coins and pottery of more than one reign or decade in it. A floor may have been laid in the reign of Vespasian, for example, A.D. 69–79. On it, as well as coins issued by that emperor, one might find straight-sided Samian bowls. The floor could have been used by the same family for 20 or 30 years before the house was altered or the floor needed to be repaired. Coins of Titus (A.D. 79–81), Domitian, his brother (A.D. 81–96), and Nerva (A.D. 96–98) might gradually accumulate on the floor. When an archaeologist studies an occupation level, as the finds on such a floor would be called, he has to look at both the earliest find and the latest in order to date the occupation. The pottery has to be studied too, and this, together with the coin evidence, would make an archaeologist decide that this floor was used in the last 10 years of the first century A.D. It has always to be remembered that the coins of Vespasian, Titus, and Domitian could have been still in circulation even after these emperors had died. In considering the date of the dumped material on this site the archaeologists had to look at the latest objects since they alone gave a firm date for its deposit on the site.

Evidence for date of forum
A white cement floor sealed the dumped material below the Roman forum. Although it had been disturbed in many areas, one part, beneath All Hallows Church, Lombard Street, was intact. Covered by the floor here were two bowls of Samian ware. This meant that they had both been deposited before building operations began. Both were in the style of the late first century A.D. One dish had the stamp of a potter who is believed to have started work in the reign of the Emperor Hadrian. This clearly establishes the forum as a second-century building, and confirms the evidence of the coin found in the mortar of the column pier.

The next building beneath the filling was associated with pottery of A.D. 60–80. The foundations of this building appeared to be aligned with a different system of streets from those

66

associated with the forum. This building would have been put up some time after the destruction of Boudicca.

Under this structure there were traces of an even older building, of which only the lowest ragstone foundations survived. This would certainly be a building of the earliest settlement at Londinium. The ragstone foundations probably had a timber structure on top.

THE DISCOVERY OF THE CRIPPLEGATE FORT

Many questions are still unanswered about the Roman defenses of London. The course of the stone wall has been studied on many occasions. The wall was approximately 2.44 meters wide. It survives in fragments and in short lengths that are visible beneath the medieval wall, which was built on top of the Roman wall. These fortifications, which were 5.5 kilometers in length, were not utterly destroyed, but survived to be rebuilt several times during the medieval period. When eventually the line of the Roman wall was abandoned and the town extended beyond it, roads and alleyways passed along its inner face. Even today it is possible to walk along its length.

There had always been one curious angle in the curved course of the wall between Bastion No. 12 and Bastion No. 15. Between the two the wall ran from north to south and then turned

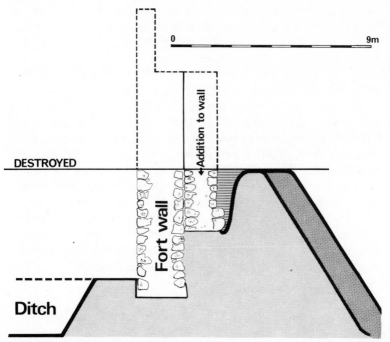

Section through the Roman fort wall showing outer ditch, foundations of both the original wall and addition to make it of the same width as the rest of the city wall.

67

Southwest corner of the Roman fort with corner watch-tower, on left; the fort wall and the later addition can be seen in the centre.

westward again before turning at Bastion No. 19, or Newgate, and proceeding to the river. An archaeologist with a trained eye was bound to account for such a curious course, which was quite unlike the gentle curve of the greater part of the wall. The Roman surveyors were logical people; they did not do such things as a mere whim. Was the ground there unsafe; did they have to avoid some natural feature such as a swamp?

Professor Grimes had the opportunity, during his work for the Roman and Medieval London Excavation Council, to find the reason for the angularity of the wall. Hampered though he was by having to allow time for his excavators to break through modern cellar floors, Professor Grimes could select points along the line of the wall at which to dig trenches. At least six cuttings were made. In spite of much robbing of the Roman levels by later builders, the course of the ditch outside the wall survived.

The wall foundations survived in many places, but the surprising fact was that there were found to be two parallel foundations in the part of the wall that lay between Bastion No. 12 and

Bastion No. 19. One foundation had no red tile bonding course as was found elsewhere in the Roman wall. It was 1.20 meters thick and made of square ragstone blocks. Inside this another wall, 1.22 meters thick, had been built. This was an addition to the narrow wall of ragstone blocks, which was later found to be a fort wall. It was unlike the typical town walls of the Romans since it was narrower and plainer. When the fort was incorporated in the town wall, the inner thickening had to be inserted.

At Bastion No. 15, on the inner side of the wall, a typical turret was found. This was a guard turret similar to those found in military forts. At this corner the double foundation ended. The fort wall turned to the east and the town wall continued as a single 2.44-meter wide wall to the riverbank. The line of the fort wall was proved to have existed from Noble Street east to Aldermanbury.

The northwestern corner of the fort was found at St. Giles Cripplegate near Bastion No. 12. From this point it was traced 193.5 meters eastward to Aldermanbury. Halfway along this

Archaeological proof of existence of fort

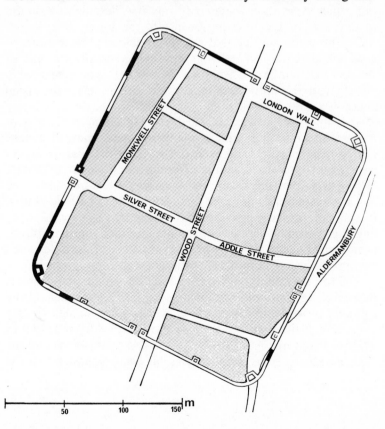

Plan of the Roman fort at Cripplegate showing how the streets reflect some of the streets within the fort.

distance the old Gate of Cripplegate had stood; this had long been considered as a Norman or late Saxon gate, but these excavations proved it to be Roman, the northern gate of the fort. Wood Street is the modern street that is roughly on the line of the north-to-south street within the fort.

The western side of the fort was 250 meters long, and the area of the whole was 4.8 hectares. This is much smaller than a Roman legionary fortress, which was more than 20.23 hectares. It was larger than the small auxiliary forts built to accommodate 500 to 1,000 men.

An opportunity occurred to examine more of the defenses when trenches were put down in Silver Street and in the area between Wood Street and London Wall. This followed the course of the east-to-west street of the fort. It was hoped that part of either the east or the west gate would have survived. A square tower on the north of the Roman street was discovered. This was the northern guard chamber of the west gate. The foundations have been preserved and can be visited (see page 104).

Further excavation was carried out at Aldermanbury on the eastern side of the fort. Fragments of the tower were found. Sufficient work was carried out to enable the excavators to ascertain that the fort defenses had existed across the line of Noble Street and Wood Street on the south. It is also reasonably certain that the north and south gates of the fort had existed under Wood Street itself.

This information was collected by painstaking recording of fragmentary evidence seen in many trenches, many dug near overhanging masonry and beneath the rubble of cellar floors. As we are only concerned with the Roman story, we are in danger of forgetting that there were many medieval features above the Roman walls and ditches. All these levels had to be cleared first. In many places, later pits obscured the sections as they had been dug through many levels. Sometimes the fort wall had disappeared completely, and only the slightest trace of the outer ditch survived to prove the position of the fort wall.

The fort appeared to have been built late in the first century. Sherds of Samian pottery buried in the earth bank behind the fort wall proved that it was not built until after A.D. 80. A very worn coin of the Emperor Vespasian, who ruled from A.D. 69 to 79, was discovered in the rubbish pit sealed by this bank. All the evidence having been considered, it has been suggested that the fort was built in the second century, between A.D. 120 and A.D. 130 in the reign of the Emperor Hadrian.

Often military forts were built in strategic positions and civilians were attracted to trade in a haphazardly formed settlement near them. When the military garrison was ordered to move to another position, the civilian town took over the area of the fort and a normal township grew up. The new fact here was that the military fort in the Cripplegate area was much later than the first civilian town.

Military garrison for the capital

Another explanation must be found to account for the existence of the fort. There must have been a reason for keeping a unit of soldiers in the town permanently. It is likely that the governor of the province had his main headquarters here. Dispatch riders would be needed constantly. Escort duties would be carried out by the unit. At Rome the emperors had their own special Praetorian Guards who were garrisoned in the capital.

Troops today guard the royal residences of the Queen and escort her on special occasions and whenever an important visitor comes to London. The Londinium garrison would have carried out similar duties in Roman times.

THE BUILDING OF THE CITY WALL

The detection of the existence of the Cripplegate fort was made possible by the study of the Roman town wall in this area. When did the defenses of Londinium become a vital problem for the ordo, or governing council, in Roman times?

At no time in its history was the settlement without some kind of boundary or some form of barrier. This was necessary in part to show where the city began because inside these limits the ordo claimed certain local taxes, while outside the area of its jurisdiction dues might be paid to the tribal territory's governing body. These boundaries may not always have been effective defenses, but it has not yet been possible for any archaeologist to make a plan of the earlier defenses of London.

Toward the end of the second century a governor of Britain called Clodius Albinus took the greater part of the army from the province to the Continent. He was trying to become emperor in Rome by defeating other candidates for the throne in battle. It has been suggested that this was the time when Londinium built its town walls, in case attack might come from unconquered natives while there were so few soldiers in the province.

It is certain, however, that the towns in Britain, whether at the beginning of, or later in, the third century, had a deliberate policy of constructing town defenses. This was actively encouraged by the emperors in Rome.

The archaeological evidence for dating the walls consists partly of two coins, one of A.D. 137, and, in a deposit sealed by bank and wall, a coin of Commodus issued in A.D. 183–84. Pottery found on the old land surface at many sites now proves that the walls were built about A.D. 200.

These defenses would consist of a wall approximately 2.5 meters thick set on foundations at least 30 centimeters wider. These consisted of large stones grouted into a firm bed. At the point where the wall could be seen at ground level, it was narrowed back to 2.5 meters. In Londinium the wall had a sandstone plinth, or lower course, and, above this, trimmed blocks of Kentish ragstone with tile bonding courses at intervals. There are two or even three lines of tiles in the bonding courses. This

Reconstruction of Londinium in the third century A.D. by A. Sorrell.

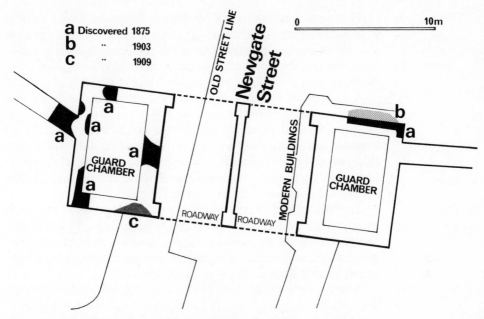

a Discovered 1875
b " 1903
c " 1909

OLD STREET LINE

Newgate Street

0 — 10m

a
a
a
a
GUARD CHAMBER
a
c

MODERN BUILDINGS

b
a
GUARD CHAMBER

ROADWAY ROADWAY

Plan of the Roman gateway at Newgate Street showing the discoveries
of different periods.

custom of putting red tiles at intervals is typical of Roman walls
whether the material was flint or the local stone.

The wall was approximately 7 meters high with a parapet
walk and crenellation at the top. The guards from the turrets
and gates could walk along the top of the wall through the
towers on either side of the gates and over the gates themselves
and could encircle the defenses without descending to ground
level.

GATES IN THE TOWN WALL

The gate that has been most thoroughly excavated is the one
that lay under Newgate Prison. Here there were two square-
fronted guard chambers on either side of a double carriageway
leading out of the town. This measured 8.5 meters between the
towers. The roads leading to the west and northwest left the
town from this gate. One continued west to Calleva (Silchester) ;
the other turned north on the line of the road known today as
Edgware Road. This continued to Verulamium and Viroconium
and after the Roman period this road was called Watling Street.　73

Gates of the
wall   The west gate of the Cripplegate fort was found during Professor Grimes' exploration. The north guard chamber can be seen in its original position below the modern street level at the west end of London Wall. The gate served the fort, as did the northern gate at the Fore Street end of Wood Street.

A gate of the Roman period was noted at Aldersgate, near the angle between the west fort wall and the town wall. Roman masonry formed curved foundations, which were the front of rounded towers flanking a gateway. There were indications that this gate had been deliberately inserted into the wall where there had been no opening before. One of the roads leading to the north left Londinium by this opening.

At Bishopsgate, Roman tiles were found embedded in rag-stone rubble and mortar. They might have formed part of the western tower of a gateway. At the junction between Worm-wood Street and Bishopsgate Street the main road to the north, called Ermine Street, left the town by this exit.

When a sewer near Aldgate, on the east side of Londinium, was excavated, part of a gate tower was found. This was of two periods, one of which might have been Roman. The main road to Camulodunum (Colchester) may have passed through this opening in the wall.

BASTIONS ATTACHED TO THE WALL

Ammunition
storage towers   Three small square towers built at the same time as the wall have been found. These were used by the guards while on watch duties and for storing ammunition. This consisted of big stones, which were hurled by large ballistae or catapults. Iron bolts were projected against the enemy by a large machine rather like a flat crossbow. These storage towers were set behind the wall.

The semicircular projecting towers or bastions, described on page 61 in connection with the Classicianus tombstone inscription, were added after the original construction of the wall. This is also the case with bastions and the walls of other towns, such as Camulodunum. As time passed, war machines changed, and instead of the lightly armed mobile troops, the army came to rely on heavier artillery machines. It needed the solid semicircular platforms on which to establish the ballistae so that stones could be hurled at the enemy. The exact date for these additions
74   is not certain, but it could have been during the fourth century

A.D., when there seems to have been a general policy of adding bastions to the walls of many towns in Britain.

The solid bastions in Londinium are on the eastern side. The bastions on the western side are different. They are hollow with narrow slitlike openings in the superstructure. This would suggest that they were used by archers. In the postwar excavations some archaeological evidence was found, but this evidence is not easy to interpret. Lying on the gravel floor of Bastion No. 14 was a coin of Constans (about A.D. 343). This was in keeping with the general belief that defenses were put in good order at that time. But doubt was again raised in the minds of archaeologists when a small stylized animal pendant was found actually on the floor. This was dated to the ninth century A.D.! It could well be that the hollow bastions were built not by the Romans but by the Saxons. It also means that Londinium was never left derelict, but when taken over by a new community, the walls were refurbished and used by defenders with a different method of warfare.

Normal Roman defenses always had a ditch on the outer side. *V-shaped ditches* This was V-shaped, as were all Roman ditches. It was 22 meters wide across the top and 5 meters deep. Although this ditch has long been filled in, its outline can still be seen in section. Excavators can see and feel the difference between the filling and the firm sloping sides of the ditch.

With a 7-meter-high masonry wall standing near the edge of the ditch there would be danger of the masonry of the wall cracking if a sufficient space were not left between the edge of the ditch and the wall foundation. So a flat piece of ground, called a berm, about 2.75 meters wide, was left between the ditch and the wall foundations.

Another part of the defenses was an earth bank piled up behind the wall. This had many uses. It may have been that the bank had existed in the position later taken by the wall before its front face was cut away and the masonry wall erected. On the other hand, the bank may have been constructed as the wall proceeded; it was built as high as the parapet walk, and it sloped downward on the inner side of the wall to reach street level. At intervals along its length there would have been steps leading up from the street level to the parapet walk at the top of the wall. If attackers brought a battering ram with them when they laid siege to the town, and supposing they managed to fill the ditch

75

and push it across to the wall, they would make little impression when there was a bank nearly 6 meters wide behind the wall to support it. The soil for the bank was obtained from the ditch and from the trench dug out for the wall foundations.

WHERE DID THE STONE AND TILE FOR THE WALL AND BASILICA, FORUM, BATH BUILDINGS, AND ALL OTHER IMPORTANT BUILDINGS IN LONDINIUM COME FROM?

In describing the wall the stone used has been called Kentish ragstone. This was natural stone quarried from rock formations near Maidstone in Kent. It had to travel some distance to Londinium, either by road or by water.

An interesting find at Blackfriars Bridge showed clearly how some at least of the stone had come to London. In the mud exposed when an underpass was being built in 1962, halfway between Blackfriars Bridge and the railway bridge, the remains of a flat-bottomed barge were discovered. The starboard side of the barge was excavated in very difficult conditions. In 1963 a further excavation was possible when a cofferdam was being built for part of the embankment wall. This was over the south end of the wreck. The boat lay about 19 meters south of the old embankment wall and under deposits of gravel and clay. Time for the excavation was so limited and was carried out under such difficulties that a mechanical grab was used to remove the gravel. A hosepipe was found to be a very effective and speedy method of exposing the waterlogged timbers. The excavators found that the barge had been strongly built of wooden planks held together by iron nails.

A copper coin for luck? A square cut or step had been made in one of the large timbers to receive the bottom of the mast. Placed in this was a worn copper coin of the Emperor Domitian (A.D. 88–89). This had been deliberately put there, presumably for luck. It is likely that an old coin was used for this deposit, which means that the boat could have been wrecked a good deal later than A.D. 88–89. In the hold of the boat was the quantity of Kentish ragstone which was its cargo.

This is how the bargemen of the second century helped bring the building material to the masons' yards in Londinium. The

76 wreck occurred toward the end of that century, a date suggested

by the shapes of pottery vessels found under the collapsed sides of the boat.

SOME OF THE BUILDINGS FOUND IN LONDINIUM

No Roman town would be complete without a public bath build- *Bath building*
ing. Because of its size and importance, there must have been
more than one in Londinium. It was usual to have one for men
and one for women in the larger towns. In small towns baths
would be open to receive women and children in the daytime
and men toward the end of the day's work and in the evening.

Baths are easily recognized when excavated since they have *Rooms in the*
to have a series of rooms, most of them equipped with furnace *bath building*
rooms and methods of allowing heat to pass under the floors.
The Romans, like all other peoples who lived along the shores of
the Mediterranean, adopted an elaborate bathing routine which
demanded several specialized rooms.

The apodyterium was the name given to the entrance hall or
undressing room. This usually stood near an open courtyard,
where the bather would first have some gentle exercise, perhaps
a ball game, to make him perspire. After leaving his clothes in a
niche in the apodyterium and paying the fee of a small bronze
coin, he passed into a heated room.

A tepidarium was the name given to a room with gentle heat
passing along channels beneath the floor. There would be hollow
box tiles set in the walls through which the hot air from the stoke-
hole would be drawn along the underfloor channels. Often these
channels would be built in a diagonal or Union Jack type of
arrangement, with diagonal channels meeting in a round hollow
under the center of the floor.

When the bather had become used to the heat and was per- *Bath routine*
spiring freely, he would pass on to a much hotter room. This
was called the caldarium. The mosaic, or tessellated, floor of this
room would be supported by a number of small pillars of tile
called pilae. These allowed hot air from the furnace rooms to
pass under every part of the floor. In the walls the hollow box
tiles were placed vertically at intervals, making flues which
allowed the hot air to pass up and out under the junction between wall and roof.

After perspiring freely for about half an hour, the bather
would be scraped all over with a strigil, a blunt, curved 77

instrument. In the curved groove dirt, perspiration, and any dead flaking skin would be removed and the bather would then splash about in hot water placed in the plunge baths built into the sides of the room.

If the bather had plenty of time to spend in the bath building, he could go into one of the small hot rooms, often round, called a sudatorium where he could sit in damp heat. Water could be poured onto the hot floor, making clouds of steam rise. When it condensed back into water, a lead or tile pipe allowed it to flow away into the elaborate network of drains that were always associated with bath buildings. In a site like Londinium the system of drains and the arrangement of the hypocaust (or underfloor heating system) rooms might be the only indications left of the former existence of a bath building.

The last stage of the bath routine would follow the final plunge into hot water. The bather would need to cool off before going out into air of normal temperature. This he did in a cool room, called the frigidarium, where he could plunge into a cold-water bath, which helped close all the pores of his skin.

In excavating a town the archaeologist always looks with suspicion on any series of heated rooms to see if they are going to form part of an elaborate public bath building or are going to be only a few rooms in the bath wing of a private house. The public baths are sure to have larger rooms than those found in a private house. They are also more certain to have several types of heated rooms. A prosperous citizen often paid a large sum of money to the local town council for the contract of maintaining a bath building. He promised to keep the fires going at the proper time and to have plenty of hot or cold water in the plunge baths. In return he made a profit out of charging admission fees to bathers.

In Lower Thames Street has been found a building with a heated double room, with curved niches or apses at opposite ends. Along the inside of the curved sides ran a tiled seat, which continued along the wall separating the two rooms. This suggests a bath building used by a number of people who would sit on the benches while undergoing their bath routine. From the evidence of the finds it does not seem to have been used after the third century A.D.

A larger building was found in Upper Thames Street. One room alone was 8 meters wide with a curved niche, again a feature typical of bath buildings. A very thick concrete foundation lay on one side. This may be the foundations of a plunge bath and all that is left of it. A terra-cotta pipe still lay in its original position leading out of the curved niche.

DESCRIPTION OF THE BILLINGSGATE BATH BUILDING

A bath building was found in Lower Thames Street at Billingsgate when the Coal Exchange was built in 1848. A room identified as a tepidarium was uncovered then and in 1859 when a group of warehouses was built in the same area two more rooms, possibly a caldarium and a frigidarium, were recorded. It was not until 1968, when recent redevelopment was taking place, that members of the City of London Archaeological Society, under the direction of Peter Marsden of the staff of the Guildhall Museum, excavated an area around these rooms sufficient to enable deductions to be made. It was established that the rooms belonged to a bath wing of a private house. A corridor lay on the north and east side of this building linking it with the rest of the house. Room (1) was the tepidarium where the bather began the heated bath. After enduring the hotter room (2) he would then have a steam bath in the sudatoria in room (3). Cooling off, scraping down, and massage were available in room (4) followed by a cold plunge at the end of room (5).

A hoard of fourth-century coins was discovered lying in the stoke-hole of the Roman baths. The latest of these coins was dated A.D. 395, which means that someone had deliberately buried his savings at a time when conditions were insecure. A further eighteen coins of the same date lay scattered on the pink mortar floor of the bath wing. The tiles from the roof had slid off the wooden framework and collapsed on this floor, providing evidence that the house was lived in until the very end of the Roman rule in Britain. The collapse of the tiles from the roof indicates that the house fell into a gradual state of ruin, for had it been destroyed deliberately there would be signs of fire.

This would be the natural place for a bath building, near the river from where water could be obtained with ease. A great number of wells have also been found in every part of Roman London. These were sometimes lined with oak planks, a number of which have now been discovered. There must also have been

Roman hypocaust and tiled seat from the bath building in Lower Thames Street.

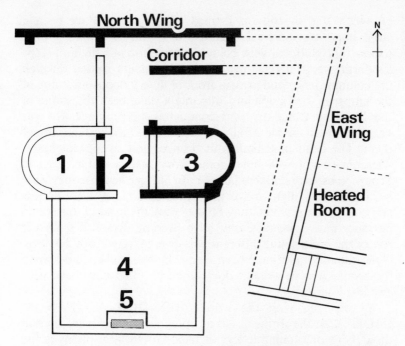

Corridor

East Wing

Heated Room

1 2 3

4

5

N

aqueducts to bring water from streams higher up the valley down to the houses.

The planning and engineering skills shown by the Romans in bringing water to a site and in constructing pipes and drains to take waste water away are very impressive. Some Roman drains are still in use today. At Bath the main outlet drain to all the water from the hot spring is of Roman construction, apart from an extension added to reach the river, since its course has changed since the Roman period.

Roman drains

TEMPLES

Just as there would have been impressive bath buildings in a town of the cosmopolitan character of Londinium, there would also have been many temples of different religious cults.

Part of a large block of stone with the best type of lettering carved on it seems to have come from a temple dedicated to the worship of an emperor, although we do not know which one. The only letters that survive are: "NUM . . . I PROV . . . I BRITA. . . ." These were arranged in three lines and the translation is "Divinity . . . Province . . . Britain. . . ." The temple

81

of which this inscription formed a part would have been a large imposing classical building. It would have had a high rectangular platform with columns at the top of a flight of steps supporting a triangular pediment. Worshipers passed through the columns to go and pray in front of a very imposing statue of the emperor. In Londinium this might have been the statue of the Emperor Claudius, who conquered the province. He was very interested in the affairs of Britain and took great care of them. The head of Claudius in bronze, now in the Colchester Museum, might well have come from such a statue. Cast in bronze, these statues were larger than life size because they were set on plinths, high above the worshipers. They were hollow and cast in parts, which may be why only the head of this statue has survived; it would easily have become detached from the rest of the body as the different parts were riveted together. Precious stones would have been set in the eye sockets, and when the bronze was new and reddish gold, it would have been very awe-inspiring.

Temple of Isis   A wine jug with the words "LONDINI AD FANUM ISIDIS" ("At the shrine of Isis at Londinium") scratched on it in the cursive or running letters of handwritten inscriptions is the only proof of the existence of a temple to the Egyptian goddess Isis in the town. The existence of the temple of an Egyptian goddess is not surprising, as merchants, sailors, and travelers from every part of the Empire must have come to Londinium from time to time. Where was the shrine itself? Up to the present, excavation has produced no indication. The Mithras temple was identified as a mithraeum because of its ground plan and because of the low-lying position of the rectangular shrine in relation to the ground around it, and would have been identified even without its sculptures. In the same way, the shrine of Isis will be recognized, if ever it is found, because it will have within its walls a special tank for holding Nile water brought from the Nile river in Egypt. Such a tank has been found at Verulamium, but not so far in Londinium. The jug with its scratched sentence must have been the property of a temple of Isis. There could well be other vessels and regalia of the cult.

Near St. Olave's Church a carved relief of the mother goddesses (deae matres) was found. This is not necessarily the site of the temple dedicated to their worship, since the carving may have been transported some distance. It must be remembered that in the latter part of the Roman period stone, whether carved or not, was seized and used in buildings of every sort, but especially in town walls and bastions. The three mother goddesses were popular deities in the western half of the Empire. In the east, Cybele was the goddess that represented the same virtues of fertility and the goddess that ensured a good harvest of all that grew from the earth. So foreign travelers could have prayed at the temple of the mother goddesses just as they would have prayed to Cybele, the earth mother. An elaborate bronze instrument, dredged up from the Thames and now on view in the British Museum, has been recognized as part of the temple property. *Cybele, goddess of fertility*

Where were the Christian churches in Londinium? It is possible that there were early Christian churches in Roman London, since the inhabitants of this port, the busiest town in the province with many foreigners coming and going, would no doubt have heard of the new Christian beliefs quicker than other places. It has already been noticed that the sculptures of the Mithras temple near Walbrook may well have been buried to save them from being damaged by Christians. It is possible, although it cannot be proved, that the actual temple was taken over by Christians and used as a church. After the conversion of the Emperor Constantine in the fourth century, there must have been Christian churches in London. Since they would belong to the fourth-century level, it is possible that they have been destroyed by later buildings; many of the buildings of the late third and fourth centuries have been almost completely destroyed. *Christianity in London*

Finds in museums help fill the gap. A pewter bowl found in Copthall Court and now in the London Museum has the Chi-

Gold medallion commemorating the arrival of Constantius Chlorus in London in A.D. 296. The top of the medallion shows the head of Constantius Chlorus himself. The reverse shows the figure of a native of London kneeling to receive the victor on horseback who had brought his troops across the Channel to reconquer the province.

Rho symbol on it. This was formed of the Greek letters *Chi* and *Rho*. These Greek letters for the first two letters of Christ's name were a symbol that Christians used when it was unsafe for them to be open about their beliefs.

Pewter was used extensively for pewter dishes and plates and for religious vessels. Ingots of pewter were found in the Thames at Battersea. These also had the Chi-Rho symbol stamped on them. Two lamps stamped with the same symbol were given to the Guildhall Museum, but these may have been brought to Britain—they are the type of lamps used in the Mediterranean.

FINDS THAT GIVE INFORMATION ABOUT THE LAST CENTURIES OF LONDINIUM

A coin with its full list of an emperor's name, style, honors, and titles written around the portrait on one side is as useful as any inscription. On the other side, the portrait of a goddess representing various virtues such as justice, security, or fortune were all part of the emperor's policy of telling all who used the coins what he was trying to do by his government and policies.

Although the foundations of many later buildings cannot be dated, hoards of coins found in the hiding places where their collectors had put them can give much information. A hoard of coins found buried under Newgate Street were all of the late third century, a time when there was much danger and insecurity. This is why the owner of the hoard had thought it wise to bury his life savings in case of attack by enemies. He never went back to find the coins, so this also is proof that he did have cause to fear. Where there are many hoards of the same period, this clearly was a time of danger.

In the late third century an official called Carausius seized power in Britain and ruled the province without authority from Rome. He seems to have been an efficient administrator and military commander. It may have been he who had new forts constructed along the east coast, which was being raided at the time by bands of Saxons from across the North Sea. These defenses were called Saxon Shore Forts and their walls still survive to a considerable height at Richborough, Pevensey, and Porchester. Carausius might well have been the first man to realize that soldiers had to be stationed near the sea. They could then take ship quickly to pursue raiders who were making life
84 unsafe in the south and east of Britain.

In London Carausius minted coins which were small copies of the official Roman coins. The portrait was not of the emperor but of Carausius himself, and, later, of his successor, Allectus. Allectus may have murdered Carausius in order to gain power. However, he was not so efficient a soldier as Carausius, and a man called Constantius Chlorus came to Britain and France at the head of an army.

A gold medallion found at Arras in France was struck to commemorate the successful arrival of the victorious Constantius at Londinium after defeating the unlawful rulers, and a copy of the medallion is now in the Guildhall Museum. On one side of the medallion is a portrait of the head and shoulders of Constantius Chlorus with his full name and title: "FL[AVIUS]. CONSTANTIUS. NOBIL[ISSIMUS]. CAESAR," which means "Flavius Constantius most noble Caesar." (He was only heir to the throne when he was sent on this mission.) *"Flavius Constantius, most noble Caesar"*

The reverse of the medallion shows the victor riding toward Londinium where a man symbolizing the citizens kneels to receive him with thankfulness. A ship filled with soldiers is shown nearby on the Thames; a gate and wall of the town are shown in the background. The letters *LON* stand for "Londinium." The other letters *PTR* below the picture indicate that it was minted at Trier in France. The lettering around the picture is: "REDDITOR LUCIS AETERNAE," meaning "The restorer of the eternal light." This shows the enthusiasm with which Britain became once more part of the Roman Empire.

No doubt, during the reign of Carausius trade had been affected to some extent. Londinium might have been able to trade with northern Europe, but the flow of exotic goods from the Mediterranean would have stopped. In other parts of Britain there was a considerable amount of rebuilding during the peace that followed this restoration. If any early-fourth-century buildings have survived under London, then they will show considerable rebuilding. The rebuilding that took place in some Roman towns in Britain shows that the building methods of the fourth century were not as good as those in the earlier periods. However, the amount of restoration already seen in other towns shows that the economy of the province was vigorous.

Even at the end of the fourth century, in the reign of Honorius, ingots of silver were officially stamped: "EX. OFFE. HONORINI," meaning "From the workshop of Honorius." 85

One 10-centimeter ingot was found in 1777 at the Tower of London. It was with a small hoard of gold coins of the reign of the same Emperor Honorius (A.D. 395–423). This does not necessarily mean that the office which stamped the ingot was near the site of the Tower or that there was still a mint in Londinium at that date.

Honorius was the emperor who wrote to the towns of Britain in A.D. 410 to tell them that they should take measures to secure their own safety. This was a surprising message, as, for 400 years, it had been against Roman law for civilians to carry arms in their own defense. The prospect of life without Roman soldiers at the Cripplegate fort or even anywhere in Britain must have seemed very strange. It was many centuries before life in London was as organized and peaceful again as it was under the Romans. The greatest skill that the Romans had brought was displayed in the planning and buildings in their towns. Since Londinium had become so wealthy and such a center for trade and government, it had become without doubt the greatest town in the province. After a considerable interval it again became the largest town in these islands, but that very activity and building have obscured and even destroyed many of the best Roman buildings.

CHAPTER FOUR

Important Finds Made in London

Apart from the extraordinary size of some of its buildings (such as the basilica at Leadenhall) and the size of the town and its fort, a survey of the finds unearthed in London would make certain facts clear. The range of pottery, glass, and personal ornaments makes it evident that in Roman times Londinium must have been a rich town. The places from which some of these items were imported show that the town had a cosmopolitan flavor.

Mention has been made above of the Arretine pottery fragments that have been found in the area of the town. While it is not possible to determine accurately whether such pottery arrived before or after the actual Roman invasion, we are now concerned only with the importing of this pottery from Italy. There is very little of it, but it does show that trade existed.

Samian, or terra sigillata, was another type of imported ware which was eagerly bought in the marketplaces in the newly founded towns. After submitting to the new Roman authority, the Celtic tribesmen in the southeast took to the Roman way of life, as we are told by the historian Tacitus. They adopted Roman dress, built Roman villas with mosaic floors for themselves, and ate and drank the things that the Roman society on the Continent had. (Tacitus mentions this in his biography of Agricola.) The love of Roman fashions is reflected in the eager way in which pottery was imported. All the towns of southern Britain have in their lowest layers the bright glossy pottery made at a place called La Graufesenque in southern France. The detection of which layers represent occupation before the attack of Boudicca and which represent buildings restored after the attack is determined mainly by an examination of this pottery. The bright-red shiny wares belong to the lowest levels. Among the range of early Samian in the Guildhall Museum is a green glazed type which is very rare and which was made at St.-Rémy

Ink well made of red Samian ware.

87

in France. Roman pottery does not normally have a glaze on it, and this one is very special as being among the few small examples that have been found in Britain.

The centers in central and northern France where Samian pottery was manufactured continued to export vast quantities of their wares to every province. The organization of middlemen who transported the goods from the kilns to the coast and then from the coast to ports in Britain was most efficient. The discovery of a shipwreck at Pudding Pan in the Thames estuary off the coast of Kent showed clearly how the pottery was brought to the port of London. In the storm which had caused the ship to sink the whole cargo of terra sigillata had gone down undamaged and lay in the mud until the pots were dredged up in 1908. This ship had been on its way up the Thames to be unloaded. The cargo would have been unloaded at the docks of Londinium and sold to different stallholders, who took their wares to markets in different parts of London and the surrounding countryside.

During the excavation of the marketplace at Viroconium (Wroxeter), stacks of Samian bowls that had been standing waiting for buyers were discovered. Because of the confusion and disaster of a fire, these bowls had fallen into the ditch and been covered with debris. One can imagine the dishes and platters from the Pudding Pan shipwreck set out on a stall in the forum of Londinium.

As time went on, the popularity of the red Samian declined. The methods of the potters and the merchants were not as efficient as they were in the early second century. Different types of beakers and bowls are found in the fourth-century levels and are on display in museums today. In the Rhineland, small drinking beakers were made and exported to different parts of the Empire. These had been dipped in a color slip (liquid color) and emerged after being fired with a dark glossy surface that made them look almost metallic. These are known as Rhenish ware.

The most characteristic shape for these beakers is a small base (often most inefficient), a bulbous body, and a neck either short or high. Occasionally there is a scroll pattern along the widest part of the bulbous body. Along the top of some of the beakers there are inscriptions: *bibe bene* ("drink well"), *misce me* ("mix me"). Presumably water was mixed with the wine.

It is even more important for us to study these imported

Stamped silver ingot, early fifth century, found on the side of the Tower of London. The lettering is "EX. OFF. HONORINI," that is the official stamp of the Imperial mint in the time of Honorius.

forms since this thin dark metallic fabric was copied by the potters in Britain. At Water Newton in the Nene Valley, not far from Peterborough, kilns began to produce beakers with similar decoration. Occasionally, instead of the conventional white slip decoration, relief patterns of leaves, shrubs, dogs, and hares were laid on the sides. Even gods or famous heroes like Hercules were shown on the sides of beakers. A very popular type of beaker was one that showed gladiators with all their different weapons and animals, lions, bears, or boars, which they fought.

Kilns of native pottery

Glass jugs, bowls, beakers, and little round bottles of every description are found on Roman town sites. Some of the more exotic jugs with twisted glass handles may have come from the Mediterranean, but many of the plain square bottles with fluted handles, which were often used to hold the cremated bones of the dead, may have come from the Rhineland in the earliest years of the Roman occupation of Britain. Later glassmakers may have come to Britain to set up their manufacturing sites and to show the local people how to blow glass. Only at Wilderspool 89 in the north and at Castor in East Anglia have sites been fully identified.

Bronze statues   The bronze head of Hadrian has been mentioned, but it is a good example of the casts that sculptors were producing in southern France and in Italy. The original statue was by a Greek sculptor; but statues were required by many centers, and the reproductions made in workshops succeeded in satisfying the demand. This head, like the one found near Colchester, was not made in Britain, but imported.

Silverware   Silver plates, jugs, and jewelry were also imported into Britain for many years. Perhaps all the best silver ware found in Britain was made abroad. The Mildenhall Hoard of silver dishes was nearly all imported, according to the experts who study works of art of this kind. It is probable that Londinium was the main port through which this "luxury trade" entered Britain.

The small silver strainer found hidden in the Mithraic temple had an elaborate container decorated with symbolic scenes of men and animals and their struggles. A griffin trying to open a box is another motif. It seems that this was a strainer for preparing a herbal drink. Was it some preparation used in the ritual of the Mithraic ceremonies? What is important is the foreign workmanship. The artist and the craftsman who had made this small object were evidently influenced by objects made in countries of the eastern Mediterranean. This is proof of the foreign elements present in Londinium. Travelers might have brought this strainer and donated it to the small mithraeum, or it could have been bought·from some eastern Mediterranean traders who had set up a stall in Londinium.

The same foreign influence was noticed on the sculptures themselves. The marble was foreign, or a workshop with foreign craftsmen working in Londinium might have produced them since the style was different from other sculptures from Britain. These are direct imports from the finest workshops of Rome.

Mosaic   Mosaic floors are another aspect that can show whether those
workers   who bought them paid a vast sum of money to an expert from abroad to come to lay a floor or whether they simply ordered a floor from the nearest workshop. It is now realized that there must have been pattern-books of floors that householders studied and then made a selection of the ones they wanted.

If there was a central design, like the circular picture of Bacchus riding on a tiger, this might be already prepared on the

90

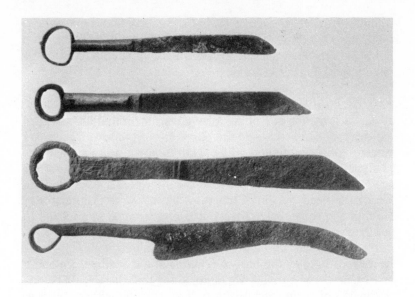

Knives from the Roman period; the second from the top is from the Walbrook area.

shelves of the mosaic worker's establishment. This would be brought to the room, and when the whole floor was measured out and the borders and subsidiary patterns were marked out, the prepared panels would be laid down on the guidelines. It does not make the craft less wonderful to suggest this method of working. There is still the art of setting out the floor, of filling in the parts between the designs and adapting it all to fit the room. The Bacchus floor was found in 1803 at Leadenhall. It might be the work of a craftsman trained abroad.

Other mosaic floors found in London show a great variety of motifs or patterns. One found at Bucklersbury in 1869 is in the Guildhall Museum. This is said to be dated to the early third century by art experts, but not by any archaeological evidence. On studying this pattern it appears that the four designs in each corner and some of the continuous guilloche, or twisted rope pattern, could have been previously prepared, but the actual design of circles and interlocking panels must have been done in the room. From the end of the first century there must have been extensive establishments in London where mosaic workers were   91 trained. From these, workers went out to lay floors not only in the elaborate houses which were eventually built inside London but also in those in the countryside, possibly in country villas as far afield as Bignor in Sussex.

FINDS IN BURIALS

It was a firm rule in Roman local government that all burials of the dead should be outside the boundary of the town. The main cemeteries of Londinium are beyond the town wall and near the main gates. Monuments were normally set out on the side of the roads so that travelers could read the inscriptions describing the life of the dead person. Cremation burials were fashionable in the first and second centuries, but later it became more usual to put the dead in coffins.

Archaeologists who find small pits containing a glass jug or a storage jar holding the burned remains of the dead person and a few other vessels, perhaps a lamp, know that this should belong to the first or second century A.D. When a coffin either of timber or of stone is found in a cemetery, it is likely that it was third or fourth century A.D. It is also a fact that if the dead person was a Christian, there will be few or no items with the body as grave goods.

If a pagan cemetery is found reasonably intact, the lamps, pottery, and jewelry found with the burials will be less damaged than the pottery found on a floor of a house or in a rubbish pit, where pottery has usually been broken in normal daily use.

One cemetery in London was discovered south of Aldgate High Street near the Minories. Its date seemed to be from the first century to the fourth, and almost all the burials were outside the wall.

Another cemetery was found in the area between Bishopsgate and extending westward to Moorgate. Both cremations and the inhumation burials were outside the wall, and in the main the finds were from the first to the third century.

Sir Christopher Wren discovered cremation burials which had lamps, flasks, and other grave goods with them in the neighborhood of St. Paul's. This area did lie outside the earlier settlements, and this is confirmed by the fact that the burials are dated to the first century. Earlier burials were found in the neighborhood of St. Martin's-le-Grand and Warwick Square. Outside the town wall at Smithfield the burials were second and early third century with some inhumations which were probably later. More burials were found in the area of the Fleet river and Newgate.

COMPLICATIONS OF THE WALBROOK STREAM

The difficulties of finding the level of the ground in the early period of the town's history have already been noted. The uneven nature of the site was further complicated by the various streams and their tributaries which flowed down to the Thames. The gradual sinking of the landmass in the southeast of England from the second century on made matters worse. Buildings in the Walbrook area did suffer from flooding. This was noted in the mithraeum, where repairs had had to be carried out within the building.

Wooden buildings, a collection of flimsy structures, suffered from flooding and were buried under the systematic leveling which took place afterward. This was the challenge which the inhabitants met and they solved the problem of the constant flooding by resurfacing floors and renewing buildings frequently. In the late second and third centuries substantial buildings were erected in certain parts of the area.

It was found after World War II, when some of the properties in this area of the city were being rebuilt, that the dampness of the old stream bed had preserved a remarkable range of small objects. These included metal objects such as are found in every Roman town—keys, latches, bronze belts, buckles, rings, pins, and brooches. Steelyards, used perhaps by merchants for weighing goods or by butchers for weighing joints of meat, were among the more interesting items. There was also an iron shackle used to fetter prisoners or slaves. A whole range of iron objects would easily be recognized by a modern blacksmith or carpenter. Tools such as hammers, saws, chisels, pincers, tongs, and billhooks do not change.

The most valuable finds to archaeologists were leather and timber objects, which had survived in very good condition because of the extremely damp site. Fragments of basketwork remind us that a good deal of this craft was practiced in the Roman period. Baskets were used by soldiers in the army, but they were used also by slaves when they did the shopping for their masters and mistresses.

Leather does not normally survive in dry levels of a site. But

Bronze phalera or ornament from the site of the Walbrook stream.

Bronze bell from the site of Bucklersbury House.

93

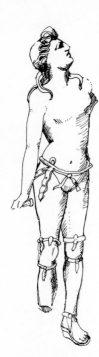

both uppers and soles of shoes were rescued during the most hectic period of the rebuilding. Some were of substantial hobnailed boots for hardworking workers and others who tramped the streets of London. Others were lighter shoes whose tops had many cutout panels and patterns. Nearly all were laced around the ankle to keep them on. But the most famous find was the small leather "bikini" type of trunks with laces to tie at both sides which was found in a well in Queen Street. This was a garment worn by girl acrobats or dancers, as shown in a mosaic found in an Italian villa.

Above: A female acrobat wearing trunks similar to those found in the well at the Walbrook. The original figure is at the Rennes Museum.

Right: Leather "bikini" from a first-century well, Queen Street.

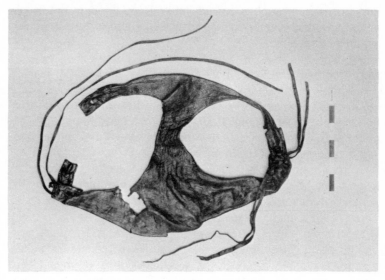

94

CHAPTER FIVE

Problems of Roman London
that Remain to Be Solved

WHO WERE THE FIRST LONDONERS?

Although it is possible to imagine the flow of people coming
from many directions to the new settlement by the bridge across
the Thames, it would be useful to know more about them. On
their arrival, the Roman government officials and army com-
manders would have conscripted some of the natives to cut
down trees in the thickly wooded areas and to transport them
to the new settlement for the erection of new buildings. Others
might have been organized into working parties to build new
roads. This would have involved digging out the foundations
and transporting heavy stones to put down before the metaled
surface was laid. The ditches on either side of the agger, or
bank, would have had to be dug out and kept clean. These able-
bodied men from the native communities would have had to
leave their homes for a while and then return when the projects
were finished.

The natives lived in communities of huts near land that could
be cultivated. Along the downland of the southern counties
they could have occupied such sites as Cissbury in Sussex.
In clearings among the forests, settlements have been found at
places such as Prae Wood, near Verulamium. These settlements
did not always have impressive banks and ditches to protect
them. By A.D. 43 they had a simple ditch or a palisade fence.
The Britons often chose marshy areas so that natural features
could be used as a protection.

During the first century B.C., before the Roman invasion of _Iron Age_
Britain, many settlements had been within strongly defended _military sites_
sites. Some were surrounded by more than one bank and ditch:
The Aubrays, near Redbourn in Hertfordshire, is one; Caesar's
Camp, Wimbledon Common, is another. The most famous of
all these sites was Wheathampstead, $9\frac{1}{2}$ kilometers from Prae
Wood in Hertfordshire. There the defensive ditch was 12 meters   95

deep. It is possible that this may have been the headquarters of Cassivellaunus, the chief of the Catuvellauni when Caesar came to Britain in 55–54 B.C.

Pre-Roman civilian communities

There must have been many more of these communities by the time the Romans came again in A.D. 43; there were many more hut sites erected and occupied outside the hill forts or the defended sites. Clearings in the forests or gravel promontories would become the site of settlements without huge defense systems. Although intertribal warfare occurred from time to time, the land around London was a little more settled than it had been. Groups may have settled on the slightly higher ground in the districts around inner London. The site of the Heathrow temple (now under a runway at London Airport) was a chance find and there may have been many other communities in the West Drayton and Hounslow districts. However, there may not have been huts in the immediate vicinity of the temple; shrines were sometimes isolated and only visited at special times of the year. To have maintained such a temple, there would have been groups of followers in the district. The map is blank at present, but it is possible that careful watch in the next few years will find Iron Age pottery and brooches or traces of huts. Pottery and brooches are the finds that will best help in the study to determine the origin of these people. Were they Belgae who were immigrants to Britain from the Continent in the second to first centuries B.C., or were some of them members of the population who were in Britain long before this time? Improved pumping machines may help archaeologists to excavate deeper and wetter levels on both sides of the Thames river where remains of Celtic settlements older than London may one day come to light.

WHERE WERE THE THEATERS AND AMPHITHEATERS OF LONDINIUM?

No Roman town was without at least one amphitheater. A town as cosmopolitan as Londinium would certainly have had one theater and one amphitheater since this was customary in all Roman towns of any size. It would not be unreasonable in a town of 54 hectares to hope to find more than one of each at some future date, possibly on the South Bank where Shakespeare's Globe theater later stood.

96   Roman Canterbury had a theater of classical plan. Traces of

the curving foundations were found in a number of cellars. Sections across the foundations had to be examined at different points and this is probably the only way in which these buildings might one day be found in London. There is now no hope of finding the building intact.

At St. Albans (Verulamium) the theater is on view to visitors today. Unlike the one at Canterbury, this is a dual-purpose building. In plan it is more than half a circle. The stage could have been used for theatrical performances, and on other occasions, animal shows could have been held in the center. This kind of economical building is found only in northern France and Britain. It would be most surprising to find a dual-purpose building of this kind in London. The great wealth of the citizens and their contacts with the Continent would have encouraged more lavish and sophisticated buildings.

A theater with a long narrow stage on the straight side and the audience sitting on the curved bank opposite may well be found in London. When it was still standing it would have looked like one half of an iced wedding cake. The outside of such buildings were heavily ornamented with pilasters and half columns, elaborate capitals, curved tops to the entrances, and passageways. It would be in the Roman tradition if an inscription were put in a prominent position to say who had built it and in whose reign this had been done. There is now little hope that much of the decoration will be preserved. Good building stone was reused several times in the Roman period and in subsequent ages. The lowest foundations alone may survive.

The actors performed on the stage against a permanent *The audience* background. In the oval-shaped amphitheater the audience sat on wooden benches on the banks all around the main arena. In Britain, even in Londinium, it is doubtful whether these buildings would resemble the elaborate stone structures in southern Gaul (France) or in northern Italy. The outer walls would be of Kentish ragstone. Tiled bonding courses would be found set at intervals in the courses of the wall in the normal Roman tradition. The best seats in the front rows, which were reserved for the members of the civil service, the governor's staff, the local council, or the leading priests, might be of tile or marble blocks. The other seats might be of timber since there were so many trees near the capital.

The animals used in the shows in the amphitheaters would   97 probably come from the Continent—bears or boars, perhaps some wolves. No lions or tigers could survive the journey and the climate. Gladiators would come chiefly from Gaul, and probably companies of traveling actors would also come from the Continent.

THE INDUSTRIAL AREA OF LONDON

Kilns were found on the site of St. Paul's Cathedral, and a brickfield appears to have existed in the area of Newgate. It was possible to find these indications of industrial activity there because this area was not built over with houses until late in the Roman period. The most densely packed occupation was in the east of Londinium. The number of kilns needed by a town the size of Londinium would have been considerable. The number and variety of types of tiles used in Roman buildings were many. The scale of the buildings in London would have kept many centers busy. Whether it is too late to hope for some further information is not certain. Sulloniacae (Brockley Hill) had kiln sites which were excavated about 30 years ago. More recently, kilns have been found in Hertfordshire near Radlett and Bricket Wood and in Highgate Woods.

It would be in keeping with the general custom of the Romans to have some kilns nearer the consumers in Londinium itself. There are clay beds in the Thames region, and kilns for both pottery and tiles should be found in these areas.

WHAT HAPPENED AFTER THE LEGIONS LEFT?

The biggest problem for any archaeologist working in London is to find out exactly what happened when organized Roman life ended in the town. It is thought that this happened at some point during the fifth century, but did occupation of the town ever really cease?

The local council, in keeping with what appears to have happened elsewhere, would have tried to maintain the security of their town. The walls would have been put into good order once more. Mercenary soldiers would have been hired to maintain these walls. (Mercenary soldiers are those who are ready to fight for any side in a war, provided they are paid and fed.) The normal citizens of towns in Roman Britain had not been allowed to carry weapons for 400 years. No wonder they felt strange and helpless when the legions had gone and they suddenly had to think of the best way to look after their own towns. This is why they hired soldiers from among people used to war.

During the first half of the fifth century some kind of order *Visit of* was maintained. Two bishops from Auxerre in France came to *Germanus of* Verulamium in A.D. 429 to discuss heresy with other church *Auxerre* leaders. Bishop Germanus and his companion must have traveled through Londinium. It seems strange to us that they could be talking about differences in church beliefs at such a time. There is a story that the bishop, who was also an efficient soldier, helped the local people fight a battle against the Picts from the far north somewhere in the region of Verulamium. The tradition is that he baptized his roughly trained followers and led them into battle telling them to shout "Allelluia." If this battle drove the enemy away from Verulamium, it would have given Londinium an interval of peace as well.

It has been suggested that these newly baptized soldiers might *Saxon* have been Saxon mercenaries. This is possible. Saxon or other *mercenaries* Germanic tribes were leaving their homes and raiding coasts and plundering for food. They were not at first concerned with finding homes for their families. The inhabitants of the towns of Britain were much more afraid of the Picts of the north, who had so often broken through Hadrian's Wall, and of the inhabitants of Ireland, who were raiding and causing much damage along the west coast. It is thought that town councils invited Saxons to fight for them against these western and northern enemies.

This may have appeared a good solution at first, but the *New settlers* Germanic fighters gradually brought their families over, and they would have settled down among the original inhabitants. Money and food would have become more scarce, and settlement may at first have been an economic solution. This may have happened so gradually that the people of the time were hardly aware of it.

If some such sequence of events did take place in the southeast, Londinium may never have been entirely abandoned. The evidence of the ornament on the floor of the hollow tower helps confirm this theory (see page 75). When further trenches are dug near the defenses of Londinium, additional ornaments, buckles, or other pieces of equipment of fifth-century soldiers may be found. It is not likely that structures will be found. At this period the huts probably were of timber, and they would have been destroyed by later medieval buildings.

The systematic exploration of cemeteries of this period will provide information. Nowadays cemeteries are being completely stripped to show all the burials. In the past only parts of burial grounds were uncovered. Cemeteries near London will be the source from which this vital information will be obtained.

It might seem hopeless to expect enough information for this transition period from a site so disturbed and built upon as London. But in archaeological investigation the search is never given up. Perhaps in some unexpected area some ancient foundation will have covered and protected some object or part of a timber hut that will provide the answer. These questions must go on being asked until the vital evidence is produced.

CHAPTER SIX

Exploring Roman London

After reading about Roman streets and buildings it is exciting to ride or walk over some of the exact area on which the Romans also rode or walked. When in a car or bus going east up Ludgate Hill, think to yourselves just before you reach St. Paul's Cathedral: *I am now inside Roman London's town wall.* As you continue down Cannon Street and come to its junction with Budge Row, remember the Walbrook stream and that as a citizen of Londinium you might have come along a street roughly on the same line and then have turned left to go to worship at the mithraeum.

As you reach the part of London between Cannon Street Station and the present site of London Bridge, imagine the heavy traffic of Roman times converging on the one point in Londinium that mattered for those crossing the river.

By turning up Gracechurch Street, the visitor today can stand at the junction with Lombard Street and Fenchurch Street and think of the traffic that has gone to the west along the line of Lombard Street since the first years of Roman rule in this island. Vespasian himself when a general could have ridden westward along it when he set out on his conquest of the south and west.

Visitors can walk for nearly 4 kilometers along most of the course of the Roman town wall and in certain parts see sections that have been exposed. In many parts, where the foundations have not actually been examined or in parts that are hidden by buildings, it may be possible to walk along a road or street on the same course that the wall took previously. This walk will take less than 2 hours.

COURSE OF THE ROMAN WALL

Tower of London

If public transport is used, Tower Hill Underground Station is the best one to use for the start of the visit. The actual wall, 101 as noted above (see pages 71–72 for description), starts on the north bank of the Thames river within the outer keep of the Tower. It is possible to see Roman masonry at the back of the ruined Wardrobe Tower of the Norman and medieval defenses. The triple courses of red tile and the squared ragstone blocks are typical Roman work. The Roman wall stands to a height of 213 centimeters in part of the bastion, above which the masonry is twelfth century. (It was not unusual for medieval builders to use Roman masonry foundations.) This bastion is shown on maps of Roman London as Bastion No. 1.

Tower Hill

A very good section of the city wall is seen above pavement level between Tower Hill and Crosswall Street. In one section the ruins of bombed cellars were cleared, and a sunken garden, made in this Roman masonry, can be seen under the medieval work. Most of the upper part of the wall here was rebuilt in the medieval period. Count the number of red bonding tiles and the number of masonry courses between them. This is the actual inner surface of the wall.

Part of an inner square turret is shown in the gardens, too. This would go up the whole height of the wall, and arms and equipment could be stored in it and used by the guards on duty.

Where the outer squared stones are missing the core of the wall can be seen.

The Classicianus Tomb

Behind Tower House, set in a modern wall that is on the same line as the Roman wall, is a cast of the fragment of the Classicianus tombstone which was found built into Bastion No. 2, which stood nearby. The cast in its setting can be seen from the parking lot behind Tower House.

Another copy of the tomb can be seen in Wakefield Gardens Tower Hill farther to the south. The statue of a Roman emperor also in the gardens is modern. To see the original fragments found in this area, ask for the Classicianus tomb in the British Museum (see pages 61–63 for its history).

All Hallows Barking Church

When leaving the station at Tower Hill, do not forget to visit
this church which has a floor of red tesserae in the crypt. This is

a second-century floor in its original position. Note that you have to descend to the crypt to see it. There are pottery and other objects on display.

In the basement of Toc H Club, 40–41 Trinity Square, a length of the Roman part of the wall has been preserved. Permission to view this may be granted if written application is made in advance to the warden. Without entering any private property the course of the wall can be followed from Trinity Square northward to Cooper's Row, where, in the yard behind 8–10 Cooper's Row at Midland House, a very impressive length is visible. The Roman section begins in the basement and extends to a height of nearly 1 meter above courtyard level. From that point upward the wall has been rebuilt, and the later masonry is not the regular lined construction of the Romans. At the top there is Norman and medieval work, even a parapet walk.

Leaving Cooper's Row, the wall continues to Jewry Street. Small lengths have been preserved in private properties here too, and special permission has to be obtained. No. 1 Crutched Friars, the Three Tuns, Jewry Street, and Sir John Cass College all have sections of the wall exposed in their cellars. Since the activities of the premises must carry on, permission to see these cannot always be granted.

Aldgate to Moorgate

The Roman wall turns west along this sector, and from under Duke's Place where Bastion No. 6 was located to the western end of London Wall, roads follow the line closely. Bevis Marks, Camomile Street, and Wormwood Street lead into London Wall. Though no sector of the wall is visible, do not forget that it was the position of the wall that caused the streets to grow here.

The core of wall visible in the north wall of All Hallows Churchyard is medieval.

Anyone parking a car in the underground garage at the western end of London Wall can see a very good section of Roman masonry extending from floor to roof. Unfortunately those on foot are not allowed to enter the garage, but immediately west of the garage are the remains of the West Gate of the Cripplegate Fort. These are open to the public between 10 a.m. and 2 p.m. Mondays to Fridays.

The Roman road to Camulodunum probably left Londinium 103

through a gate at Aldgate, though no foundations of the gate have been found. Through Bishop's Gate Ermine Street, leading north to Durovigutum (Godmanchester), most probably left the City. If you wish to explore the area around London, it would be possible to follow their course to some of these places.

Cripplegate Fort around London Wall

As mentioned above, Wood Street and Silver Street are probably on the same lines as streets of the fort. If you walk north along Wood Street before its junction with Fore Street, the northern gate of the fort will have been crossed. But it lies many feet under the pavement—even supposing the masonry has been left there and not taken away.

The masonry of the fort defenses was discovered to the south, not very far from the point where Love Lane turns away from Wood Street.

To return to the visible sections, the most exciting view can be obtained from the upper pedestrian way north of the new London Wall. Stand near St. Alphage Churchyard; from there the eastern end of the wall can be seen. It shows two separate foundations. The fort wall, 1.5 meters wide, is the outer one, and inside stands the wall that was added to make the fort wall the same width as the city wall elsewhere.

Walk along to see the northwestern corner bastion of the Roman defenses from the same parapet. This is that dramatic corner where the whole of the defenses turns sharply south. This had been suspected even before Professor Grimes discovered the fort wall. The bastion that can be seen in part here is No. 15, the corner bastion of the fort.

A culvert for conducting waste water away from the buildings in the area can be seen cutting through the wall at ground level.

Under this again there is the sloping side of the ditch of the fort. This was one of the things about the fort that helped Professor Grimes follow the line of the fort defenses. This part of the ditch cutting into the natural soil has been left open so that visitors can see the evidence. But it must be remembered that the Romans had filled the ditch in completely before they built the wall at this point.

Aldersgate to Blackfriars Lane

104   A visitor to the course of the Roman wall should write for per-

City wall, at St. Alphage churchyard, with double Roman wall at base (fort wall on right, later addition on left).

mission to visit Bastion No. 19, which was discovered beneath the yard of the General Post Office in King Edward Street. Letters should be addressed: The Post Master, The GPO, St. Martin's-le-Grand. By going down a ladder from the level of the yard to the bottom of the bastion, the change of level between the modern London and Roman London is dramatically brought out.

The wide and busy road of Newgate Street lies above the foundations of the double gateway with the square tower on each side that was found beneath Newgate Prison. This is the gate that stood on the line of Watling Street, the main road to the northwest.

By walking down the road of Old Bailey, the course of the wall can be followed in a straight line—the foundations stand to the east of this modern road. To see the actual line, it is better to walk down Warwick Lane, which is well within the wall area, 105 then to turn into Amen Court, since the wall is under the foundations on the western side of the court.

From this point the wall is known to run directly down to the riverbank at Queen Victoria Street near Blackfriars Station. Test areas have been dug, but the determined visitor who wants to complete the course must walk along Blackfriars Lane and look down the alleyways to the east to remind himself of the line of the wall.

EXPEDITIONS TO SEE BUILDINGS WITHIN LONDINIUM

The Temple of Mithras that was excavated so carefully by Professor Grimes was taken up from its original position and has been relaid on a raised platform on a terrace outside Temple Court at 11 Queen Victoria Street. It is about 50 meters away from where it was found and was relaid lying north–south although it had been built lying east–west. It must also be remembered that modern flagstones have been put on the floor of the shrine. The various floors of the original temple were of earth or mortar. It is interesting to be able to see the plan of the building. Lower Thames Street was the site of a small bathhouse which might have been used by the general public. Permission for small groups of visitors can be obtained from the keeper of the Guildhall Museum, but no visits can be arranged for weekends, when the building is completely closed. A wall with a tiled seat in front of it and part of one of the hypocaust buildings have been preserved.

ROMAN BUILDING OUTSIDE THE WALL OF THE TOWN

The only certain building found outside the wall of Londinium stands under part of St. Bride's Church in Fleet Street. Part of a plain red tessellated floor ran under the apse of the first church. It is reasonably certain that many such buildings did once exist outside the line of the wall.

MUSEUMS WITH OBJECTS FROM LONDINIUM

Walking along the line of the wall and visiting the actual buildings of Roman London are exciting, but to understand the subject properly, visits must be made to several museums to see 106 some of the objects which have been discussed.

Guildhall Museum

Roman objects from the area of the City of London are in the Guildhall Museum. It is at present in Gillett House in Basinghall Street. There you can view the finds from the Mithraic temple, as well as a whole range of objects of every material—bronze, pottery and leather—used by ordinary people living in Roman London. There are also cases which give news of the latest discoveries made by the staff and the City of London Archaeological Society.

London Museum, Kensington Palace

It is well worth the walk to that part of Kensington Palace that houses the collections of the antiquities of London found outside the small area of the City. Here some of the sculptured stones found in the unorganized period of early-nineteenth-century excavations are on view. The different kinds of other pottery brought to Roman London and used there are set out in the cases. These, when studied with the objects in the Guildhall Museum, will complete your picture of the many different activities of the citizens of Roman London. The Guildhall and London Museums will be amalgamated by 1975 in a new building at the junction of Aldersgate Street and London Wall.

Time Chart

55–54 B.C. Julius Caesar invaded Britain and in 54 B.C. crossed the Thames river.

A.D. 43. The Emperor Claudius planned an invasion and made Britain a province of the Empire.

A.D. 61. The attack on Londinium by Boudicca. Following this disaster the town was rebuilt and some years later the Procurator Classicianus was buried near it, thus proving that it was an administrative center at this early date.

A.D. 122–25. The Emperor Hadrian visited Britain and encouraged civic building as well as the supervision of the frontier in the north of England.

A.D. 196. Clodius Albinus, the Provincial Governor, took the legions to the Continent when he tried to become emperor and much damage was caused to the towns of Britain by barbarian raiders from the north.

A.D. 268–. Carausius, a government official appointed to keep the English Channel free from pirates, took possession of Britain and ruled it independently of the imperial authority.

A.D. 293. Constantius Chlorus was sent by the emperors to reconquer Britain and to carry out extensive rebuilding programs.

A.D. 312. Constantine the Great, son of Constantius Chlorus, decreed that Christianity should be recognized as the religion of the Empire.

A.D. 367. Count Theodosius was sent to Britain to restore order after extensive damage by barbarian raiders. Throughout the fourth century London remained a flourishing commercial center in spite of repeated attacks.

Suggestions for Further Reading

The following books provide a starting point for further study.

General reading on Roman Britain:

A. Birley, *A Life in Roman Britain* (Putnam)
Bruce Collingwood, *Handbook for the Roman Wall* (Andrew Reid)
L. Cottrell, *Seeing Roman Britain* (Pan Books)
I. A. Richmond, *Roman Britain* (Penguin)
L. Rivet, *Town and Country in Roman Britain* (Penguin)

Books on Roman London:

D. R. Dudley and G. Webster, *Rebellion of Boudicca* (Routledge)
D. R. Dudley and G. Webster, *The Roman Conquest of Britain* (Batsford)
W. F. Grimes, *The Excavations of Roman and Medieval London* (Routledge)
W. F. Grimes, *Recent Archaeological Excavations in Britain* (1956 Ed. Bruce Mitford)
R. Merrifield, *The Roman City of London* (E. Benn), 1965
R. Merrifield, *Roman London*
Roman Finds from Bucklersbury House (Guildhall Museum, London)
H. Young, *Roman London* (London Museum/HMSO)

Reports and journals:

Transactions of the London and Middlesex Archaeological Societies. Various reports from the founding of the journal—notable numbers are:
P. Marsden, "Excavations of a Roman Barge at Blackfriars," Vol. 22, Part 2. Archaeological Finds in the City of London 1966–68.
K. M. Kenyon, "Excavations in Southwark (1945–47)." *Transactions of the Surrey Archaeological Society*, No. 5, 1959.

Antiquaries Journal:
G. C. Dunning, "Two Fires of Roman London," *Antiquaries Journal*, Vol. XXV, 1945

Current issues of the *London Archaeologist*. These contain reports on recent excavations in London

Royal Commission on Historical Monuments (England), *An Inventory of the Historical Monuments in London,* Vol. III, *Roman London in 1928*. This book is long out of print and can only be read in libraries.

More advanced books on Roman Britain:

S. Frere, *Britannia: A History of Roman Britain* (Routledge)
J. Liversidge, *Britain in the Roman Empire* (Routledge)
J. Toynbee, *Art in Roman Britain* (Phaidon Press, London)

WEIGHTS AND MEASURES
METRIC AND ENGLISH EQUIVALENTS

1 meter	= 1.0936143 yards
1 kilometer	= 0.621371 mile
1 sq. meter	= 10.76393 sq. feet
1 hectare	= 2.47106 acres
1 litre	= 1.75985 pints
1 gram	= 0.03215 ounce

Index

111

112